Some of you might know Wil Anderson as 'the one in the middle on that ABC TV show with the weird name' (*The Gruen Transfer*); or 'the one who wasn't Corinne or Hughesy on that show that used to get in trouble all the time' (*The Glass House*); or maybe even 'the guy who hosts *Spicks and Specks*' (that's actually Adam Hills but he gets that a lot).

You might have also heard him on the radio playing the 'Wil' part of *Wil and Lehmo* on Triple M, a show that was described by one critic as 'being on at the same time as *Hamish and Andy*'. For five years he also got up at a time most people consider 'last night' to be 'the one who knew lots about *Buffy* but nothing about maths' on the much-loved *Triple J Breakfast Show* with Adam Spencer.

Wil also does a bit of writing, and for the last six years has written a regular column for the *Sunday Magazine* (*Herald-Sun*/*Sunday Telegraph*). He can happily boast that his first best-selling book, *Survival of the Dumbest*, is 'over 250 pages without pictures'.

But it is stand-up comedy that is Wil's true passion. He has proudly told 'dick jokes for cash' in pretty much every comedy club and festival in Australia, he's taken his knob gags international at all the major festivals from Edinburgh to Auckland to Montreal, and he's graced some of the most famous stages in the world in New York and LA.

In 2008, Wil was named *GQ*'s Comedic Talent of the Year, and given an excellent trophy, which he immediately misplaced while drunk at the afterparty.

wilanderson.com.au

Also by Wil Anderson
Survival of the Dumbest

FRIENDLY FIRE

WIL ANDERSON

EBURY PRESS

An Ebury Press book
Published by Random House Australia Pty Ltd
Level 3, 100 Pacific Highway, North Sydney NSW 2060
www.randomhouse.com.au

First published by Ebury Press in 2009

Copyright © Wil Anderson 2009

The moral right of the author has been asserted.

All rights reserved. No part of this book may be reproduced or transmitted by any person or entity, including internet search engines or retailers, in any form or by any means, electronic or mechanical, including photocopying (except under the statutory exceptions provisions of the Australian *Copyright Act 1968*), recording, scanning or by any information storage and retrieval system without the prior written permission of Random House Australia.

Addresses for companies within the Random House Group can be found at www.randomhouse.com.au/offices

National Library of Australia
Cataloguing-in-Publication Entry

    Anderson, Wil, 1974–.
    Friendly fire.

    ISBN 978 1 74166 926 8 (pbk).

    Australian wit and humor.

    A828.4

Cover design by Christabella Designs
Cover photographs by James Demitri
Internal design by Midland Typesetters
Typeset in Bembo by Midland Typesetters, Australia
Printed and bound by Griffin Press, South Australia

Random House Australia uses papers that are natural, renewable and recyclable products and made from wood grown in sustainable forests. The logging and manufacturing processes are expected to conform to the environmental regulations of the country of origin.

10 9 8 7 6 5 4 3 2 1

For Nerija and Richard

CONTENTS

one and what do you do?	1
two the old and the beautiful	31
three doing it for the kids	59
four something old, something new, something borrowed, something blue	93
five aussie aussie aussie, eh eh eh	135
six romancing the stoned	171
seven survival of the fattest	201

ONE
AND WHAT DO YOU DO?

Sometimes I suspect that when I was a kid my parents dropped me on my head and something broke in my brain.

The thought occurred to me while celebrating Easter this year, when a ridiculous question formed inside my noggin: before Jesus rose again, did he push the snooze button and say, 'Ah, screw it. Ten more minutes, who will know?'

You might think this isn't a big deal, but this is the crap that preoccupies me.

Over the years I have lost count of the ridiculous rubbish that runs rampant through my brain: when librarians die do they get buried according to the Dewey decimal system? If 'upskirting' is looking up someone's skirt, what does that make 'updating'? And don't even get me started on 'downloading'.

Do 'Weird Al' Yankovic parody acts sing the original versions of the songs? Is there any easier job in the world than a professional wrestling referee? Step one: learn rules. Step two: ignore rules.

If you had a mental condition that stopped you from using any form of electricity, would you be known as the Barmy Amish? And more importantly, during Earth Hour did those with OCD turn their lights off, then turn them back on again, then turn them off, then . . .

It takes only the smallest thing to set my brain off on a flight of fancy, and I can lose half the day. Recently, for example, I was listening to the radio when the newsreader reported that AC/DC tickets were 'selling like hotcakes'.

Really? I thought. Like hotcakes? Is there someone in this country who is selling 100,000 hotcakes in half an hour (for $150 bucks each)? I'm clearly in the wrong game.

I started wishing the rest of the report had been: 'AC/DC tickets are selling like hotcakes . . . for four bucks at Maccas, but only before 10.30.'

In fact, the radio tends to trigger my brain into Burke and Wills-style wanderings quite often. For instance, every time I hear that NASA has sent an 'unmanned probe' into space, it sounds less to me like a rocket and more like something lesbians might use to get pregnant.

And my brain isn't better served by TV. The other night I was watching a fascinating documentary about the guy called the Tree Man. Do you remember him? He had a disease that made him look like a tree. It was an amazing doco full of drama, courage and medical miracles, but as usual I missed all this because I was more fascinated by the fact that the Tree Man's teenage son was an emo.

Yes, that's right. Suddenly my brain was filled with questions: if your dad is the Tree Man and you are an emo, does that make you a treemo? Or maybe an Elmo?

When the Tree Man's emo son cuts himself, does he use a chainsaw? Does he bleed sap? Is the son ever referred to as 'a chip off the old block'?

But it's not just the Tree Man. I couldn't watch *Ladette to Lady* without thinking that it would be much more entertaining the other way around: if they'd got a bunch of posh, frigid chicks and sluttied them up a bit.

Speaking of reality TV, according to *The Biggest Loser* Club ads, all you have to do is 'replace two meals a day'. Okay, that seems fine, but what about the other seven?

Even when someone tells me good news my brain still takes the logic road less travelled. The other day I heard that advertising course enrolments had gone up 30 percent since the beginning of my show, *The Gruen Transfer*. Now this should have filled me with pride, but all I could think was: 'Wow, imagine the effect of *Underbelly* on those who want to get into organised crime!'

The other day I was in a pie shop that claimed it sold 'award-winning pies'. Clearly, I should have busied myself sampling these famous pies, but instead I was paralysed, wondering how it can be that every pie shop I ever enter seems to sell 'award-winning pies'. For a start, how do the pie-makers find time to actually make pies in between attending all those awards ceremonies?

You might dismiss all this as inconsequential; after all, what's wrong with looking at the world in a slightly askew manner? And I agree, to a point. I quite like that when I left some money in the ATM recently, I didn't get upset at losing the cash but decided it was my version of the stimulus package and I was helping to end the recession.

I love that when I see the moon out during the day, my initial thought is that it's pulled an all-nighter and decided to go straight through. (And I often sneak a second look to check if it's eating a kebab.)

On the other hand, I do sometimes wonder how much I could achieve if my brain worked like a normal person's and I didn't waste my time wishing there'd been a *Carry On* movie called *Carry-On Baggage*.

Imagine the diseases I might have cured if I'd spent my time studying science instead of doing things like writing a letter to the AFL suggesting that if they truly wanted to honour Anzac Day, they'd get the British to send the Pies and Bombers to the wrong ground, and then get them to play uphill in the mud?

Who knows, I could have been the next Stephen Hawking if my brain were as fascinated by physics as it is by worrying that now that *Big Brother* has been cancelled, my sexual euphemism 'visiting the rewards room' will never catch on.

And wouldn't the world be better off if my waking thoughts were dedicated to unlocking the key to world hunger rather than wishing *O, The Oprah Magazine* was more like Oprah, so one month it would be fat, the next month thin, the following month a bumper edition?

Sadly, however, I seem stuck with this slightly offbeat view of the world and no matter how hard I try, the nonsense continues to spill out. Just this morning I walked past a couple of dog owners who were trying to pull their pets apart. A tiny Shih tzu had tried to attack a Great Dane. The owners looked at me in despair, their eyes pleading for help, but all I could think to mutter was: 'Typical tall puppy syndrome!'

I rest my case.

So I have nothing but admiration for those people who have disciplined minds and engage in meaningful and worthwhile endeavours.

In fact, if I were prime minister for a day, the first thing I'd do – after putting on my Aussie tracksuit and passing a law that says Cate Blanchett has to marry me – would be to give teachers and nurses a pay rise. It doesn't say much for our society when a stripper who performs as a sexy schoolteacher or naughty nurse gets paid more than the people who do those jobs for real. Of course, if there are any kiddies reading this, I should point out this does not mean the next time Miss Jones bends over to pick up the chalk in biology you should try to slip your lunch money into her garter belt.

I'd even go so far as to say that the jobs of teaching and nursing should be completely tax-free – or at the very least, we should provide teachers and nurses with the phone number of Kerry Packer's former accountant. (If I had my way, kids wouldn't just bring apples for their teachers, they'd bring them iPods.)

But all jokes aside, I truly do believe that teaching is the most noble and important job in the world, and it really pisses me off that sometimes we treat teachers as though the only qualification you need to teach Grade 2 is to have passed Grade 3. 'Mr Jones, it says on your CV that you excelled at colouring, and were in the top percentage of your class in T-ball, bootball, handball and rounders . . . You can start on Monday!'

Look, I'm not saying all teachers are great. There are certainly a few who found their way into it not through a love of nurturing the next generation, but through a love of having six weeks off at Christmas. I had one teacher who was so bored, he used to stand up at the front of the class and sniff the whiteboard markers all day long. On the upside, he did always give me great marks and said I was one of the smartest pink lizards he had ever taught.

I know this will come as a real shock to most of you, but I was a bit of a brat at school. Almost every report card I received contained the comment, 'Wil will do well in life, as long as he stops trying to be funny all the time!' (I suspect some of my former high school teachers might be working in ABC management these days.)

My major problem at school was boredom. In most humanities, arts and language classes I had more As than a Queenslander making a speech, but in maths and science I scored so many Cs my report card sounded like a Spanish couple on their wedding night.

In Year 10 maths, I remember being so uninterested that I would sit up the back of the room, tear up my textbooks and throw them into the ceiling fan. And when they scattered down I would get everyone to sing Christmas carols.

In science, my mates and I spent most classes seeing how many things we could turn into bongs. (Which meant we did great on the practical, but not so good on the theory.) And even back then I would constantly get in trouble for things I said. In one class, the teacher was so frustrated by my questions she snapped, 'Well, if you think you can do a better job, why don't you come up here and teach the class?'

So I did. I immediately sent her to the principal's office, cancelled all the homework and took everyone on an excursion to the pub.

I almost got expelled on my last day of school. You see, at my school, there was a tradition among Year 12s to parody the daily school bulletin. Unfortunately, my version of *The Bull Sheet* proved a bit much for some of the teachers I'd targeted, and they demanded I be kicked out. Imagine that:

me getting into hot water for making fun of those in power. Lucky I grew out of that.

Even back then I knew I wanted to make people laugh for a living; I just didn't know how. And that's where teachers can be so important. The good ones encourage kids to follow their dreams, and I was lucky enough to have some really inspirational ones – Mr Simons, Mrs Ethridge, Mrs Weir, Mr Cowling and Robin Williams. Oh hang on, I'm thinking of *Dead Poets Society*.

But while a good teacher can inspire you, a bad one can scar you for life. When I told one teacher – let's call her 'Mrs Brown' – that I wanted to tell jokes, she told me that it was never going to happen. That day, I went home in tears.

It was years later that I finally found the courage to follow my dreams. A few more years after that, Dave, Corinne and I were sitting around trying to come up with a name for our TV show. We finally settled on *The Glass House*, but I must admit I wanted to call it *Stick It Up Your Arse Mrs Brown*, so that every week when she opened the newspaper she'd see that she was wrong.

Sometimes I still have to pinch myself when I realise I get to tell jokes for a living. This year I celebrated my fourteenth year at the Melbourne International Comedy Festival.

I knew I was getting older when last year a new comic came up to me after a gig and said, 'Hey, you're Wil Anderson. I used to watch you on TV when I was a kid!'

When . . . he . . . was . . . a . . . kid? Ah, that must have been one of my regular appearances on Graham Kennedy's *IMT*; I wonder how I looked in black and white? Oh well, I guess anything that took his mind off the dinosaurs wandering around outside.

But I must confess, as I prepared for the start of my tenth MICF show – i.e. flicked through *Kochie's Best Jokes* and searched the back of public toilet doors for witty graffiti – it did seem a long time since I'd lost my festival virginity.

And believe me, doing a show for the first time is a lot like 'doing it' for the first time. For starters, you're usually drunk, and the first thing you realise is, it's nowhere near as easy as it looks in the movies. You're trying your best to make the other person feel great but, despite your various efforts, most of the time your rhythm is completely out and it's awkward and disappointing. There are whole routines that you blow prematurely and other jokes you can't get up no matter how hard you try – although on the upside, if the audience fakes it you can't tell the difference.

In fact, looking back on it, the only real difference between my first festival show and the first time I made love is that at my show *they* were paying *me*. Oh, and I let my mum and dad come and watch.

If I'm honest, Mum and Dad were about the only people who *did* come. You know that old saying, 'If you only make one person laugh ...'? Well, that could have been the review of my first Comedy Festival season. I was performing in a broom cupboard in the Melbourne Town Hall, and I couldn't even fill that room. On my opening night two people attended, which meant that taxidrivers bringing people to the Town Hall had bigger audiences than I did.

However, on the second night things really turned around when four people came to the show. I felt like Big Kev, by which I mean excited, not dead. Obviously the word was getting out there. The buzz was spreading. I'd already doubled my audience. I figured that if this happened each night, by the end of the month I'd be the biggest act in the festival, with TV and movie deals and even my own range of aftershave called Smells Funny.

Then on the third night, tragedy struck. I had no bookings at all, so I was forced to stand out the front of the Town Hall with flyers, begging passing strangers to come to my show.

In this situation it's hard to know what the best pitch is. After all, nobody knows – or cares – who you are, so I tried everything from, 'Please take a flyer; if I can't have your money, your pity will do' to 'Come to the show and you can sleep with your favourite cast member.' In the end, the only way I could get people to take them was to say, 'These flyers are made with incredibly cheap chemicals, and if you lick them you'll get high.'

When I got really desperate, I decided to try flyering the line of some other shows, like *Puppetry of the Penis*. Not that I have anything against the lads from POTP; I actually supported them once. (When I say 'supported', I mean I told some jokes before they came on stage. I didn't hold anything out of the way while they were trying to manipulate their downstairs parts into a mini Sydney Opera House.)

I decided on a little spiel: 'Hey, after you've seen some knobs, how about some knob jokes?'

People were just turning away and looking down their noses at me in disdain. I was so tempted to snap at them, 'You've just paid thirty bucks to spend an hour watching some blokes play with their peckers until they resemble the Leaning Tower of Piza. I'm sorry I offended you, Your Majesties!'

I was reminded of this experience recently when I attended the Edinburgh Fringe Festival. For those not familiar with the Edinburgh Fringe, it goes for a month, more than a thousand acts perform, and the average audience size is seven. So you can see it's not exactly a money-making exercise. I probably could have stayed at home and flushed my wallet down the toilet each day and still have come out ahead.

To get people to come to your show is a combination of good word of mouth and hard work. Like most acts, I would spend at least two hours a day on the street handing out flyers and basically begging people to come. I have to confess I got really bored, so to keep myself amused, I'd set little challenges.

My favourite was the day I decided to only target men with beards. I thought it would be fun to have an audience that looked like an audition for *Braveheart 2: Drunk and Drunker*. I was also tickled by the idea of the beardy blokes looking around thinking, 'Wow, maybe I'm right. Maybe the beard is coming back. I wonder if these guys also like ZZ Top?'

Anway, I was hoping to get a nice crowd of forty or fifty on the first night and try to build it from there. When I walked out and was greeted by a crowd of more than two hundred, I thought I'd accidentally walked into someone else's show. As it turned out, opening night was also half-price tickets night, so the room was filled with Aussie tight-arses – sorry, backpackers. Don't get me wrong, it was amazing to have them in, I was just slightly annoyed I had spent thirty hours on a plane taking all the local references out of my show, when I could have kept them in and just had four confused Scottish people saying, 'What's a Shannon Noll? And more importantly, can you deep-fry it?'

It's fair to say I didn't make much money at the festival, largely because of the shocking exchange rate. In the UK, the Aussie version of *Who Wants to Be a Millionaire?* would be called *Who Wants to Win Three English Pounds?*

Seriously, everything I bought cost three times what it usually does. It was like living in a giant hotel minibar. (On the upside, at least it gave me a taste of the future.) One day, I gave the dude at the currency booth AU$100 and the exchange rate was so bad I didn't get anything back. In fact, he said I still owed him money.

Come to think of it, it might've been better to have been paid in drugs – at least they would have kept their value. Don't scoff: it happens all the time. Once, when I first started out in comedy, the promoter came up to me after a gig and said, 'Look, we don't have any money for you, would you like to be paid in drugs?'

As a naïve 22-year-old, my first thought was, 'What, a couple of Panadol and some Metamucil?' Then I realised he was talking about the harder stuff. That's when it struck me that I definitely wasn't working for the *Financial Review* anymore. And for a minute I have to confess I did think about it. Not because I wanted the drugs, but just to feel for one second like I was in Mötley Crüe.

Because, while it saddens me to admit it, when it comes to comparing rock and roll and comedy, stand-up does not stand up. For starters, rock and roll is cool. Everyone knows the old saying, 'sex, drugs and rock and roll'. Comedy is more like 'sex jokes and getting the dole'.

And before we move on, as Salt and Pepa would say, let's talk about sex. There is no doubt that rock and roll is much sexier than stand-up comedy. Despite girls often listing 'sense of humour' as an attractive quality, you rarely see them getting randy for John Candy. A male rock star can get a round of applause just for taking his shirt off. Let's face it, there are rock drummers who I don't think have even owned a shirt. A comedy gig is about the only place you'll hear an audience member scream, 'Put your shirt back on!'

Rock and roll stars get groupies. The only groupies comedians get are people who book their tickets in groups so they can get a discount.

But while it makes me jealous, I totally understand this. Music can be incredibly moving. It can connect with something deep inside your soul (and sometimes a little lower). You rarely see a comedy gig where people wave their lighters in the air and couples gaze into each other's eyes and say, 'Oh, this is *our* knob gag!' I've been to a lot of weddings, and have yet to see the bridal waltz performed to Dave Hughes's 'Snakes Alive' bit.

Plus, music can make things sexy. You can take someone home, dim the lights, light some candles, slip on some Marvin Gaye, and let's . . . get . . . it . . . on. I somehow doubt you'd get the same effect if the CD was Ugly Dave Grey.

Rock can also make you angry or sad and people will happily pay to feel that way. If you do a stand-up comedy gig and people feel sad and angry by the end, they'll probably demand their money back. You certainly wouldn't be able to justify it by saying, 'Oh no, I'm an emo-comedian!'

But it's more than the capacity for emotional connection that gives rock the advantage over jokes. It's timelessness. If a band or singer writes a great song it can live on forever – and people will want to hear it over and over again. When you're in rock and roll, no-one wants to hear the crappy new album, they want to hear the hits. The Rolling Stones don't walk on stage, launch into 'Start Me Up', and have people scream, 'Heard it! Get some new stuff!'

Every comedian would love to be able to walk on stage and say, 'This is a routine that has been great to me over the years, I hope you like it too. It's called "Klim is milk spelled backwards".' A comedian can never stop in the middle of a routine, point the microphone towards the audience and yell out, 'Come on . . . you know the words!'

And if you're a rock and roll star, you can make an impassioned political speech before you introduce a song and the crowd will go wild and lap up every word. This doesn't work for comedy at all. You never see a comedian start a bit with, 'There's been a lot of talk about this next song, maybe too much talk, but this song is not a rebel song, this song is . . . "Rootin' in the Back of the Ute!"'

Rock and roll really has it over comedy when it comes to manners, too. Rock and roll is all about rotten behaviour and rebellion. A rock star can throw a TV out the window of a hotel room and people think it's cool. If a comedian tried the same thing people would think, 'Wow, he's definitely not going to get his bond back!' Is it asking too much to allow me, just once, to throw a TV out a hotel window? That's all I ask. Although, being a comedian, I'd probably ruin the coolness of it by explaining that I did it because there was a Daryl Somers special on.

In rock and roll, it's expected that the musicians behave as offensively as possible, but the same leeway isn't extended to the punters. In fact, I reckon we need a special version of the Ten Commandments just for gigs.

Now before I go on, I should clarify that I'm not a religious person; nevertheless, I like the idea of existence coming with a detailed set of instructions. If you think about it, the Commandments are like God's version of 'Life for Dummies'. My only gripe with them is that they're not detailed enough. As life gets increasingly complex, surely it's time for the Big Fella Upstairs to upsize the list?

Here's a case in point: the other night I went to a concert and the guy in front of me hoisted his girlfriend onto his shoulders, thereby completely obscuring my view of the band I'd shelled out seventy bucks to see. I wished I'd had a Ten Commandments of Appropriate Behaviour at Gigs. If nothing else, I could have thrown it at the inconsiderate idiots to get them out of my way.

But perhaps I'm being a little demanding of God, expecting him to come up with gig commandments. After all, these days it seems the Big Fella has his hands full helping sportspeople win races and rappers win Grammys. So I asked my mates and the general public for their views, and here, in the name of making this crazy thing called life just a little simpler, are my Ten Commandments for Concerts.

Commandment One: If you want to have a conversation with someone, do it at the bar or, better still, at home.

Seriously folks, what are these people thinking? 'Wow. I really need to spend some quality time with Mark in deep and meaningful conversation. Better get us some tickets to Rage Against the Machine'?

Commandment Two: If you're going to the mosh pit, finish your beverage first. Remember, if you drink and mosh you are a wet, sticky idiot.

Commandment Three: If you are going to sit on your boyfriend's shoulders, improving your view of the stage but obscuring it for half the audience, please take off your top so at least the crowd has something interesting to look at.

Commandment Four: Apart from the aforementioned shoulders commandment, shirts should remain on at all times.

The obvious exception is if you are the band's drummer, in which case being topless at all times during the gig is compulsory.

Commandment Five: If you are going to follow the lead singer's exhortation to 'put your hands in the air' and then 'wave them like you just don't care', please make sure you have first applied a liberal amount of deodorant.

Commandment Six: If you must take photos, try to avoid pointing the flash in the artists' eyes.

Nobody wants to hear, 'It was an awesome gig last night ... I managed to give Phil Collins a seizure!' (OK, maybe a couple of people would be happy to hear that one.)

Commandment Seven: You must be 100 percent sure of the lyrics before committing to singing along.

The worst example of this was when I went to see Rick Springfield – don't ask – and ended up standing next to a woman who kept singing that she wished she had Jessie's squirrel.

If you do plan to sing along, the rule with volume is simple: you should never sing so loud that the person next to you hears you more than the artists they shelled out fifty bucks to see. The only exception to this rule is when the lead singer invites you to sing along by using phrases such as, 'All together now', 'Come on, you know the words' and 'Am I ever gonna see your face again?'

Commandment Eight: When attending a gig you must not, and I stress *must not*, wear a T-shirt featuring the band you are actually seeing.

This is particularly bad if you have just purchased the T-shirt at the merchandise desk and are now sitting on your boyfriend's shoulders.

Commandment Nine: If you don't have fluorescent green hair in your everyday life, don't dye it fluorescent green for a concert.

Chances are, sometime in the middle of the show the dye will start to mix with your sweat and run down your face. You'll end up looking like The Hulk's love-child.

And last but not least:

Commandment Ten: Earplugs should not be worn at any time. If it's too loud, you are too old – go home.

The only exception is if you happen to find yourself at a James Blunt concert, in which case feel free to use earplugs, earmuffs, or chop off your ears if need be. Yes, I have high standards and can't tolerate listening to or watching anything that is boring, dull-witted, unimaginative or dumb.

Which is what a few critics labelled Baz Luhrmann's latest film, *Australia*; but I have to say, I didn't mind it. (Although I can't help thinking, if it were truly a movie about Australia, it would have been made by a bloke called Bazza Luhrmann and called *Straya!*) When the film was first released, there were lots of rumours (denied by Baz) that he was forced to give the movie a happy ending after a test audience didn't respond well to the original one. (Apparently, in the original downer ending it was revealed that Hugh Jackman had been dead the whole time and was just a ghost being seen by the Aboriginal kid; and then Nicole Kidman took off her clothes and she was really a man.)

I have to confess that I was initially offended by the idea that the fabulous Mr Luhrmann, an internationally renowned and successful artist, might have been forced to change his vision just because a bunch of people who had nothing better to do with their day than to see a movie in exchange for a piece of free pizza and some cask wine said he should.

In fact, I was more than offended, I was outraged. He is an artist! Who has the right to tell him what his vision should be? Surely a storyteller should be left to tell the story? I mean, did someone lean over Leonardo da Vinci's shoulder when he was painting the *Mona Lisa* and say, 'Look, it's pretty good Leo, but couldn't you have got her to smile? Seriously dude, just before you did the mouth you should have shouted, "Say cheese!"'

Did someone say to Ken Done, 'Hey Ken, how about you try painting something other than koalas, the Opera House and the Harbour Bridge?' (OK, maybe that's a bad example.)

But the more I thought about it, the more I started to think the test monkeys were right. I mean, who really wants to go to the movies to be moved, challenged and have their thoughts provoked? Not me. If I want that I'll go down to the local art-house cinema and watch a movie about an Uzbekistani farmer and his existential relationship with a goat.

When I go to the movies I want some escapism and to eat a bucket of overpriced popcorn, not to have to read subtitles. I want to watch some stuff blow up and then see the heroes live happily ever after. I'm still pissed off that there were no awesome car chases in *Driving Miss Daisy*.

But why stop at giving *Australia* a happy ending? I mean,

AND WHAT DO YOU DO?

everyone loves a happy ending (although occasionally it does cost a little extra). Why not re-edit some other so-called hit movies to give them the happy endings they deserve.

Take one of Baz's other movies, *Romeo and Juliet*. Now that was a great movie – Leo and Claire, guns and violence and music. But what a bummer ending! I know it was based on a play by some old dude called William Shakespeare or David Williamson or something, but did they really have to die at the end?

Surely Juliet could have discovered Romeo had poisoned himself and given him CPR while ringing the poison advisory hotline for some information? The paramedics could have pumped his stomach and they could have lived happily ever after, popping out really cute kids. At the very least, it would have meant there could have been a sequel.

And what about *Titanic*? I know it's the highest-grossing film of all time, but what a sucky ending. Surely Kate Winslet could have scooted over a little on that wardrobe door and let Leo on as well? Or was she worried about having enough leg room to do her exercises so she wouldn't get deep-vein thrombosis?

In fact, why did the boat even have to hit the iceberg? It could have narrowly missed thanks to some great stunt-driving by the captain (who, in the remastered version, would be played by Sandra Bullock) and Leo and Kate could have bonked the whole way. It would have been like a big-budget *Love Boat*.

While we're talking blockbusters, like many people I loved the movie *King Kong*, but did the monkey have to die at the end? Couldn't they have trained him, waxed him, and got him a nice little studio apartment on the Upper East Side? He would have made an excellent fifth cast member in *Sex and the City*.

There are so many movies that would be better with a happy ending. Don't tell me *Bambi* wouldn't be a better movie if Bambi's mum had just got a flesh wound. Or if in *Weekend at Bernie's* it turned out that Bernie was just a really heavy sleeper? Or if Patrick Swayze had stayed in Whoopi at the end of *Ghost* and got it on with Demi Moore? Or if in *Gallipoli* the Aussies had won? Or if in *Thelma & Louise* they managed to do an awesome donut off the cliff and the cops let them drive to Mexico?

Million Dollar Baby would be a much better movie if it ended with her becoming champion of the world. *Brokeback Mountain* would have won more awards if Heath and Jake had opened a B&B together. And I wouldn't be scarred for life if, at the end of *The Crying Game*, she took off her clothes and was just a really hot naked chick.

Then there are the scary films like *Wolf Creek* which, as well as not having a wolf or a creek in the entire movie as far as I could tell, also had a pretty downer ending. It would have been a much better film if the backpackers had actually befriended Mick Taylor and ended up running an outback car repair service.

AND WHAT DO YOU DO?

And don't even get me started on *Jaws*. That movie scared the crap out of me. I couldn't go near the beach for ages. Instead of a scary shark, why couldn't Jaws have been a friendly dolphin who solved crimes like Flipper?

Like a lot of people, I judged *Trainspotting* to be a pretty good movie, but to be honest I thought it was ruined by all the sex, violence and drug-taking. Surely they could have gotten rid of that stuff and just made a really nice movie about people who like trains?

And it's not just modern movies that need a re-edit; some so-called classics also have rubbish endings. Like *Casablanca*. I mean, that is a great movie – amazing actors, memorable lines – but you can't tell me it wouldn't be even more fondly remembered if Ingrid Bergman had stayed with Humphrey Bogart and they'd teamed up with Sam to turn Rick's Café into Rick's Karaoke Bar.

Some critics have called *Citizen Kane* the greatest film of all time, but what the hell do critics know? All that stuff about Rosebud being his sled – that was rubbish. It should have been revealed that Rosebud was where his family had their holiday house when he was a kid.

And I know people seem to have a sort of enduring affection for the movie *Gone with the Wind*, but I reckon it would have been a much better movie if at the end Clark Gable had said, 'Frankly, my dear, I do give a damn . . . in fact, you had me at hello!'

Yep, I've seen a few movies in my life; it's my favourite

form of escapism. I love nothing more than to walk into a darkened theatre, bucket of popcorn and Coke in hand, and immerse myself in a totally different universe. These days I (reluctantly) accept the difference between the made-up and real worlds; but when I was growing up, I always wished my life was more like the movies.

I remember watching films as a teenager and thinking how amazing it would be if you really could transform the ugliest girl in school to the prettiest, simply by shaking out her ponytail and taking off her glasses. Think of all the body-image issues and eating disorders you could immediately resolve by throwing away the specs and banning the bun! (And wouldn't it make a great episode of *Extreme Makeover* if, instead of the usual plucking, sucking, fat-dumping and breast-pumping, contestants were simply told, 'OK four-eyes, take off the glasses and shake out the scrunchie . . . and we're done!')

In real life, the girl would only become irresistible to people turned on by chicks with messy hair constantly bumping into things.

Movies can be dangerous and misleading for kids. Growing up watching American films, I assumed all high-school janitors were either trustworthy confidants and companions (kind of like counsellors who put sawdust on vomit in their spare time) or misunderstood maths geniuses.

Sadly, most of the time they revealed themselves to be creepy old guys who were absolutely no help at all with homework or emotional problems, and weren't safe to be

AND WHAT DO YOU DO?

alone with in their sheds. (A shed, I should point out, that was most likely being used to store cleaning supplies and manufacture methamphetamine.)

When I was a teenager, I certainly wished fights resembled those in the movies. In any action film, no matter how many villains attack the hero, they always join the fight one at a time – kind of like they've taken a ticket for the deli at Coles and are waiting their turn. In my playground, the other kids obviously hadn't read their movie-fight rules of engagement, because they'd all punch and kick me at the same time. Then a couple of them would hold me down while another spat in my mouth. This never happens to Jackie Chan.

And while I'm on the subject of high school, what about the prom? In all the movies about high school I grew up watching, all dilemmas, problems and major plotlines are resolved at the prom.

Watching American teen movies, one could be mistaken for thinking that they held a prom every second week, yet I didn't experience a single prom in my entire six years of high school. Sure, we had blue-light discos, but you can't resolve a problem at such occasions, especially something as complex as a bet that you can turn the ugliest girl in school into the most popular.

Movies are misleading on more than just the big issues; the small stuff always seems easier, too. For instance, phone calls seem much simpler. No time for g'days, hellos or random small chat, it's always straight to the point and then you just hang up – no need for goodbyes or I'll-message-you-in-the-mornings.

I would have been hopeless in a movie. 'Well, there you go, there's all the important information you need to save the world, so I guess I should go then . . . no, you hang up . . . no, you hang up . . . no . . . you . . . hang . . . up. OK, on the count of three we'll hang up together. One, two, three . . . you didn't hang up!'

The same applies to catching taxis. In a movie, the hero can be in the middle of an intense chase scene, jump in a cab, shout 'Follow that car!' and not only travel the whole journey without once saying, 'So mate, you been busy tonight?' but at the end always have the exact change for the trip.

I'd make a horrible movie hero. I'd be chasing the baddie and when the cab pulled up I'd say, 'Sorry mate, can you change a fifty? It's all I have. You can't? Damn . . . OK, maybe I have something smaller in my pocket. Damn . . . I know, I'll use my Eftpos card. What's that? Your machine is on the fritz . . . OK, I'll tell you what, I'll leave my stuff here and just duck inside the house and get some change . . .'

And in movies, if you can't catch a cab, don't worry. Because any movie hero (or villain, for that matter) worth their salt can hotwire a car and have it started within three seconds. I am still constantly amazed by this, because I can't start my car in less than a minute and I have the keys. And that doesn't count the time I spend adjusting the seat, mirrors and radio station.

AND WHAT DO YOU DO?

Don't even get me started on movie musicals. I've lost count of the number of times I've tried singing and dancing at the local 7-Eleven and, instead of joining in, everyone has just stared at me as though I was the crazy one. It's enough to drive you to drink. In fact, bartender, can I have a scotch on the rocks please? Screw it, just leave the whole bottle. What do you mean you can't leave the bottle without a deposit? They do it all the time in the movies!

But sometimes truth is stranger than fiction. Even in the movies, it would be considered far-fetched for the American people to have voted not once but *twice* for George W. Bush to be their commander-in-chief. Unless, of course, the movie was a comedy.

You see, while Dubya is widely acknowledged to have been one of the worst presidents in the history of the USA, he was an absolute godsend for comics. After all, this is a man who once said, 'Rarely is the question asked: is our children learning?' (Although technically, I guess you have to admit he is right. That question is rarely asked. A more frequently asked question is, 'How the hell did we elect a president who even Forrest Gump would have made fun of at school?')

I guess this really shouldn't come as a surprise from a man who also said, 'You teach a child to read, and he or she will be able to pass a literacy test.' Ah yes, George W. Bush giving advice about literacy. It's kind of like getting abstinence advice from George Michael, or Amy Winehouse suggesting you 'just say no to drugs'.

In his heyday, the man was a comic genius. At an economic conference he once said, 'I promise you I will listen to what has been said here, even though I wasn't here.' He is either a complete moron or one of the most provocative existential thinkers of our time. (It's one of the great philosophical questions: if a tree falls in the forest and only George W. Bush sees it, was he really there?)

That's not to say he didn't also understand the plight of the battler. I mean, this is the leader who in 2000 said, 'I know how hard it is for you to put food on your family!' And it's probably a little kinky and unhygienic too.

But say what you like about the big bad Bush, he was a believer in families. In 2000, he said, 'Families is where our nation finds hope, where wings take dream!' What the . . . ? Put it this way, you know your presidency is in trouble when Yoda could give you grammar advice.

And Bush was not just a man of words; he was also a man of action. In 2001, he noted, 'For every fatal shooting, there were roughly three non-fatal shootings. And folks, this is unacceptable in America. It's just unacceptable. And we're going to do something about it.' Too right, compulsory target practice in schools . . . with the added benefit of keeping class sizes down.

Anyhoo, you see my point. When it came to making life easy for comedians, the man was a gift, and we thought we would never see his like again. But then along came Sarah Palin, the woman who even dumb blondes made jokes about.

AND WHAT DO YOU DO?

Sarah Palin, who, when asked what magazines she read, said, 'All of them!' Well, I'm sure the boys at *Zoo Weekly* will be rapt to hear that their 3-D Bootylicious Babes edition played such a pivotal role in American politics.

Sarah Palin, who claimed she had foreign policy experience because she could see Russia from her house. That's like me claiming to be a horticulturalist because I can see a tree out my backyard window. I had to shoo a stray dog out of my front yard the other day; that doesn't make me a vet.

Sarah Palin, the pitbull with lipstick, whose nickname during the presidential campaign should have been 'pap' given the amount of smearing she did. She even accused Barack Obama of 'palling around with terrorists'. What next, revealing that he'd been in an '80s covers band called Obamarama?

Sarah Palin, who, when she was governor of Alaska, abused her power by firing the state police chief because he wouldn't fire her sister's ex-husband. I'm sure he voted for Obama, because if Palin had won, the ex would have been sent on an all-expenses-paid holiday . . . to Guantánamo Bay.

And my absolute favourite: Sarah Palin, who admitted she believed the dinosaurs were in the Garden of Eden with Adam and Eve. Hmmm, I think Sarah might be getting the Bible confused with *The Flintstones*. I don't think I remember that bit in the Good Book when Eve says, 'Hey Adam, do you want an apple?' And he replies, 'I yabba dabba do!'

TWO

THE OLD AND THE BEAUTIFUL

I turned thiry-five recently which, touch wood, should mean I'm only about halfway through my life. People tell me I shouldn't feel too old; after all, they — and they would know — say thirty is the new twenty. (Especially when you're talking about the exchange rate of the Australian dollar overseas.)

OK, I think the expression is actually 'sixty is the new fifty', but most people who say this are baby boomers hopped up on Ugly Dave Grey's nasal spray.

However, if sixty is the new fifty, then it surely follows that fifty is the new forty, forty is the new thirty, thirty is the new twenty, twenty is the new teenage, and ten is the new newborn. (Although it is a little more awkward if you are still breastfeeding.)

So, according to this logic, I only just turned twenty-five. The bad news is, my twenty-year-old girlfriend is now only ten and I'm in a hell of a lot of trouble with the authorities.

But if this is my 'true' age, why does it feel like the extended warranty on my body ran out a couple of years ago, and since then everything has started to fall apart? (And you think it's hard to get spare parts for a second-hand European car?)

I first began to notice it when something as simple as moving started to come with its own soundtrack. Five years ago, when I got out of bed it was done silently. These days it's accompanied with a groan that sounds halfway between a Hungarian weightlifter completing the clean and jerk and a phone call that should be charged at $4.95 per minute.

Lying on the couch is still relaxing, but trying to get back up again takes so much out of me that I need another lie-down. The cruellest twist is, now that it takes me twice as long to get off the couch to go to the toilet, my bladder has decided I need to urinate twice as often.

And can someone please explain why when most men hit their mid-thirties they start to lose hair from the place they most need it (on their head, keeping it warm) and grow it in places they don't? You'll be happy to know that this winter, while the top of my noggin is suffering frostbite, the insides of my ears are going to be snug as a bug. If I want to conceal my receding hairline, I'm afraid the only solution might be to grow my nose hair really long and comb it back over.

As if to add insult to injury, at thirty-five years of age what little testosterone I have floating around my body has finally decided to kick in, and I have started growing chest hair. Not Tom Selleck/*Magnum, P.I.* chest hair, though. No, I have the chest hair equivalent of bumfluff. To give you the image, it kind of looks like a four-year-old has tried to make a beard for a Santa card using only cottonwool and Clag. Oh yes, hello ladies . . .

So now I have to decide what to do with it. There's too much there to ignore, but nowhere near enough to keep. Do I go all Mr Miyagi and wax on, wax off? That seems a bit extreme given how few hairs there are – kind of like using napalm to clear up the cockroaches under your fridge. I guess I could pluck them individually ('she loves you, she loves you not, she loves you'). Or perhaps I could ring Advanced Hair Studio to see if they go 'Yeah, yeah' to chest hair?

But wait, there's more. As well as my hair, I'm losing my eyesight. On the upside, it makes it harder for me to see my bald patch. Now, to be completely frank, the eyesight thing is not that new. It's been getting progressively worse for about the last five years. When I was thirty I had 20/20 vision; now when I watch the Twenty20 cricket on telly I need a pair of glasses that even Kevin Rudd would think are a 'bit nerdy'. Put it this way, you know your eyesight is getting worse when you need to find your glasses so you can find your glasses.

But it turns out that losing my mobility, hair and eyesight is the least of my worries. I went to the doctor the other day because I was having some unusual headaches, only for him to examine me, turn to me solemnly and say, 'I have some bad news, Mr Anderson . . . you're losing your hearing.'

I said, 'What?'

He repeated himself, this time a little louder and emphasising each syllable: 'You . . . are . . . lose . . . ing . . . your . . . hear . . . ing!'

'I know,' I said. 'I heard you the first time, I've just always wanted to do that gag.'

As it turns out, it's no joking matter. I am actually losing my hearing. I have a condition called tinnitus, which is basically a ringing in the ears. The good news is, I have now stopped saying to strangers, 'Could you answer that, please?' The bad news is, there's no real cure.

'Are you sure?' I asked when the news finally settled in. 'I mean, I've been growing a lot of hair in my ears lately. Maybe it's just getting in the way.'

No, tinnitus was the diagnosis. Most likely caused by years of standing too close to the speakers at rock concerts, and listening to music too loud in my headphones at radio stations. Of all the things that are going wrong, that one sucks the most. Because if you think about it, he was basically telling me that I've ruined my hearing by hearing things too well. I mean, that sucks butt like it was involved in a butt-sucking competition in Buttsuckia.

I'm glad this doesn't happen with the other senses. Imagine eating a really good meal and then completely losing your sense of taste. Or walking past a bakery in the morning and losing your sense of smell! Suddenly the newspapers would be filled with reports that Stevie Wonder had 20/20 eyesight until he watched the leg-crossing scene in *Basic Instinct*. Or that George W. Bush had once had 'one really good idea'.

But the thing that really made me feel old – aside from having to finally admit to myself that it's pretty unlikely I'll ever play cricket for Australia – was when some of my well-meaning (read 'idiot') friends decided to take me nightclubbing.

Now, the first thing I need to point out is I've never really enjoyed going to nightclubs, even when I was younger. I'm more of a pub man. In fact, there are baby seals who like clubbing more than I do.

The second thing to note is that these days, going clubbing is not as simple as rocking up to a bar for a couple of drinks. Oh no, it's more like an off-your-face amazing race where, by the end of the night, I had so many nightclub stamps down my arm it looked like I'd been sharing a cell with Chopper Read.

Although, on the upside, it is really handy the next day when you have a hangover and are trying to piece together just exactly what you did the night before. (And believe me, you will have a hangover. These days kids don't sip drinks, they scull them as if alcohol is being banned at midnight.)

The next thing you need to know is that nightclubs these days have better light and smoke shows than Mötley Crüe do.

At one club there was so much smoke I felt like I was partying in John Elliott's lung.

While that might seem cool to the kids, people in their thirties don't go to nightclubs to see a laser-light show. They're more likely to get laser eye surgery. And most people in their thirties don't need to go out to a club to have someone babble incoherently at them and then vomit; they just stay at home with the baby.

Then there's the music. While I still dig a great loud rock gig, I've always had the sneaking suspicion that the music in nightclubs is only loud because if conversation were audible, the people who go to those clubs would never have sex again.

And there's nothing more guaranteed to make you feel old than someone trying to pretend they're up-to-date with music when they're clearly not. In the space of half an hour I had one mate describe emo as 'that Elmo music' and another enthuse about the remix of the dance track that was playing, until we all realised it was actually the fire alarm.

But forget the smoke, lights and music, the thing that made me feel like I should have been at home receiving my telegram from the Queen were the other punters. Put it this way, you know you don't quite belong when everyone in the club is staring at you because they think you're either an undercover cop or have just popped in to pick up your kids.

All the girls seemed to be very forgetful, too. First, they had forgotten they weren't yet eighteen but had gone out to a nightclub anyway. (Seriously folks, I have T-shirts older than most of the people who were in the room.) Then, most of them had forgotten to wear pants. I honestly felt like telling them to put something on before they caught a cold. I've been to strip-clubs where the girls wear more. One look and Sheik al-Hilali's head would have exploded.

And let's not forget the boys, who are skilfully able to drink and dance while keeping the waist of their jeans at the perfect point – about halfway between their waist and their knees. Now, I've been known to wear the occasional pair of low-slung jeans, but I felt like Harry Highpants compared to these blokes. They had them slung so low they didn't have to bother pulling them down to go to toilet.

When I looked at these kids, I realised that no matter how hard I pretended, we came from different worlds. When I was their age, Michael Jackson was black, George Michael was straight and Dannii was the most famous of the Minogues.

In my time, Australians were actually proud to say that Mel Gibson was our countryman. (Although, let's face it, he's drunk and racist: what could be more Aussie than that?) I come from a time when the only ice available at a nightclub was sitting at the bottom of a glass of Midori and lemonade, and an age when the only Hilton a teenage boy dreamed about spending a night in was a hotel.

It was time to face facts. Thirty was not the new twenty, and I was getting older. Which would be fine – after all, I'd been looking forward to that wisdom you're supposed to get as you accumulate the years. But for me, the complete opposite seems to have happened. Forget *Are You Smarter Than a 5th Grader?* I'd struggle on *Are You Smarter Than a Rugby League Player?*

For starters, I've completely lost touch with popular culture. When someone told me recently that Chris Brown was in trouble for abusing Rihanna, I honestly said, 'Really? But he seems so nice to the animals on *Bondi Vet*.' When someone else asked me if I was outraged about the lesbian storyline on *Home and Away*, I must admit I blurted out, 'The only thing that shocked me was that it didn't involve Irene.'

Technology seems to be passing me by, too. When a mate told me the other night that he was tired from staying up all night playing with his Wii, I told him I wasn't judging but I didn't want to hear about his perverted fantasies. When he explained it was a computer game console and he'd just bought *Don King Boxing*, I added insult to injury by saying, 'Oh, I wouldn't want to play that, all the fights would be fixed!'

But I'm not just losing touch, I also seem to be slowly losing my mind. Like the other night, when I ended up going to bed with a pen still in my pocket. I woke up the next morning with scribbles and ink stains all over my new sheets. It looked like I'd had a torrid affair with Mr Squiggle.

I also seem to have lost quality control over my mouth. I was having a security system put in at my house recently and the guy installing it told me that to prevent the cats setting it off, it wouldn't detect anything under thirty kilograms. Instead of expressing my appreciation of this useful feature, all I could think to say was, 'But what if my house is robbed by midgets . . . or supermodels?'

I'm honestly starting to think that when my dentist removed my wisdom teeth recently he made a mistake and removed my wisdom. Consider this. Occasionally, when I think of an idea for a column or a joke and I don't have a pen handy, I send myself a text message. But of late I've noticed that seconds after I send the message my phone will beep and I'll think, 'Oh, a text message. I wonder who that's from?'

And then at Easter time, one of the newspapers put out their weekend edition (which covered Friday and Saturday) on a Friday, which I bought and read. Only problem being, I then bought and read it again on the Saturday, thinking that it seemed familiar; I wondered whether I'd developed psychic powers in my sleep.

Even when something nice is happening to me, I manage to absentmindedly bugger it up. The other day I went to have a massage and facial I'd been given as a gift, but got there a little early and decided to grab a falafel roll. Only problem was, it was filled with garlic, so for the next hour I couldn't enjoy my massage because every time the masseuse came anywhere near my face I had to inhale and hold my breath. Furthermore, she kept asking me questions I couldn't answer. I didn't know what was worse: having her think that I was rude or that I stank.

To pour lemon juice into the paper cut, later that night at dinner, still a bit light-headed and wobbly from the massage, I knocked over the salt, spilling it all over the table.

'Don't worry,' my dinner companion proclaimed, 'just throw it over your shoulder, it's good luck!'

Thinking I could desperately do with a change of luck, I grabbed a handful of the white gold and flung it over my left shoulder . . . right into the eye of the person at the next table. So it may have been good luck for me, but the same couldn't be said for the person behind me who was now blind. (Luckily they didn't see it was me, as they seemed to have something in their eye.)

It is becoming clear to me that the more likely the situation is to be publicly embarrassing, the more my brain will let me down. Like the other day, when I had to give a urine sample while having a medical. Now, it's true, given that most blokes have trouble aiming into a regular toilet bowl, giving us a tiny little jar seems to me a tad optimistic. But as I wandered back into the doc's office, holding a cup of what I was trying desperately to pretend was warm apple juice, the doctor shocked me by saying, 'Well done!'

Well done? I mean thanks, but it's not like I managed to sign my name in the snow. What was I meant to reply to that? All I could think to say was, 'Thanks . . . I made it myself!'

Clearly my mouth and brain – which used to work reasonably well together – have had irreconcilable differences and decided to part company. The final straw came during a recent blackout when I popped next door to find out if my neighbours' power, gas or water were working. Well, that was my intention. But when they opened the door, the first words I said were, 'Hey, do you have gas?'

I'm not just getting more stupid, I'm getting more emotional too. After a recent tough patch I found myself crying at least once a day for almost six weeks. Put it this way, you know something's going a bit pear-shaped when even the cats start staring at you like, 'Crap, we're going to have to start building an ark!' It got to the point where every time a pizza delivery boy arrived at the house I had to pretend I'd just been cutting onions, or watching the end of *The English Patient*.

I was also having a lot of trouble sleeping. And I started walking in my sleep – one morning I woke up in the spare room. Well, I assume that means I'd been walking in my sleep; that or I had a fight with myself during the night and had to sleep in the other bed.

My nights became a combination of half-sleep, half-dream, and I found myself staying up for hours worrying about the tiniest and strangest things. One night I tossed and turned endlessly, seriously struggling to understand why pizza shops charge you extra for an added ingredient but don't reduce the cost if you want something removed. I mean, surely if it costs another dollar for extra anchovies, if I *don't* want anchovies they should take off a buck? Right? Anyone?

If you think worrying about that is stupid – and fair enough – wait, there's more. The following night my z's were interrupted by thoughts about ads on radio. If a radio station does an ad-free hour of songs, but then interrupts it every five minutes to tell you they're not playing ads, isn't that just as annoying? 'All right, you're listening to our ad-free fifty: fifty songs in a row with no ads in between apart from this annoying voice-over constantly telling you that we don't play any ads!'

The next night it was even more bizarre. I couldn't sleep because I was worrying about how much money it's appropriate to contribute towards a gift for someone you don't know. You see, at my work that day someone was leaving and a card and collection went around the office. Now, I'm all for chipping in, but I didn't know this person. Plus, they were leaving so I'd never get to know them. More importantly, they'd never get to know me and contribute to a pressie when I got the arse!

Sometimes my insomnia was prompted by the last thing I'd watched on the telly before I hit the sack. One night I spent about five hours staring at the roof wondering why beer ads always seem to feature disco tongues and blokes planting hair and growing pod people. I mean, why don't they just tell the truth? 'Beer: it tastes delicious and makes other people more interesting and more likely to sleep with you!'

Another night I made the mistake of watching the lotto draw before beddie-byes and spent the next few hours obsessed with why, when people win Tattslotto, they say, 'I'm not going to let it change me!' You know what? If you're not going to let it change you, then don't enter. If you're completely happy with your life, let the rest of us losers get the chance to live in a gold house and drive around in a fur car.

People often talk about running in their dreams, but in my case it was driving. In my weird night-visions, I was stuck in traffic behind a truck which had a bumper sticker saying, 'Don't follow me . . . I'm going fishing!' And all I could think was: 'Well, what if I fancy a spot of fishing . . . can I follow you then?'

Speaking of driving, another thing that drives me mad is wondering why people feel the need to spend heaps of money on personalised numberplates that say the brand of their car. The other day I saw a red BMW with the number plate 'REDBMW'. Yeah, I'm guessing if you can't work that out using your eyes, you probably can't read the numberplate. It's like spending $1000 on a T-shirt that says 'T-shirt'.

My sleeplessness was making me mental. Every night at the exact moment my head hit the pillow, it seemed to fill with questions. Like, why do people feel the need to talk in movies? The only time it's appropriate is if they're the director and doing a live director's commentary.

And why are people compelled to rub the bellies of pregnant women, even if they don't know them? Do they think that if they rub hard enough a genie will pop out and grant them three wishes? (And while I'm on the topic, why is it appropriate to rub the tummy of a pregnant woman, but if you try the same thing with a hot girl in a bikini suddenly the authorities get involved?)

As if all these anxieties weren't enough, one night, just after stepping out of a warm shower before I hit the sack, I discovered that the hairs on one side of my chest had started growing longer than the ones on the other side. Well, there went that night's slumber: I tossed and turned, worrying about whether I should get my chest waxed or just grow the hair on one side really long and comb it over.

I finally decided I needed to talk to somebody about it. So I started thinking: if you have a problem, and no-one else can help, who do you call? Then I realised that was the theme from *The A-Team*, and probably wasn't that helpful. I decided to go and visit a counsellor instead.

Now, as an Aussie bloke, this was a pretty tough thing to do, to walk through a stranger's door and say, 'I need some help!' (Particularly as the first time I tried it I had the wrong address and startled an elderly couple in their living room.)

But my counsellor was really lovely, and really helpful, and for a few months I popped in once a week for an hour to spill the beans on everything from life to love to work. My radio partner Lehmo teased that if I talked about him, he should get to book the session straight after and have the right of reply.

Despite the sessions sometimes being very hard work, there were a bunch of little things about my weekly appointment that brought a smile to my face. Like the fact that for the first few weeks I couldn't shake the nagging feeling that my counsellor reminded me of someone. Then, as I sat there one week I realised who it was: Jessica Fletcher from the TV series, *Murder, She Wrote*. I couldn't help thinking of her as some sort of super-counsellor who solved people's emotional problems by day and solved mysteries by night.

The other thing I found amusing was that the counsellor's office had no couch. Now, if Hollywood movies have taught me anything apart from the fact that any nerdy girl at school can become the Prom Queen by taking off her glasses and shaking out her hair, it's that when you go to a shrink you lie on a couch. Forget the pub with no beer, I went to the counsellor with no couch.

Well, technically that's not exactly true. She had a little two-seater, but when I tried to lie on it my legs stuck over the end like I was a backpacker dossing on a sofa in Earl's Court.

Then there were the notes. While I talked, my counsellor took notes, which I assumed was pretty standard psychiatric *shtick*. But then I became completely obsessed by what she chose to write down and what she didn't.

I was trying to talk honestly about my emotional issues, but all I could think about was, 'Why didn't she write down anything when I told her about my PE teacher who used to pull his pants down to his ankles when he used the urinal, but couldn't stop writing when I told her I found the Brand Power lady a bit hot?'

But the thing I loved most about my counsellor was her wicked sense of humour. After all, they do say that laughter is the best medicine – although I have to be honest with you,

I prefer drugs. I've lost count of the number of times I have lain in a park hoping someone would plant drugs on me.

But I digress.

It might seem weird for someone who does what I do for a living, but during my post-birthday slump there was a time when I forgot how wonderful it is to laugh out loud. Then one day after I'd spilled a particularly emotional story and was feeling very sorry for myself, my counsellor just looked at me and said, 'Isn't this funny?'

I was taken aback for a moment, looked up, wiped the tears from my eyes (I hadn't been crying, I had been watching *The English Patient* while cutting onions) and asked softly, 'What? What is funny about this?'

She just smiled and said, 'Well, normally people pay to listen to you talk . . . but you have to pay me!'

My counsellor wasn't the only person I was paying to get myself in better shape. As well as my deteriorating mental health, I was starting to notice that my physical body was also in a state of serious decline. It got so bad that when taking my shirt off at the beach, I wasn't so much worried about rubbing on sunscreen but about Japanese tourists covering me in wasabi and soy. One day someone even asked me if Wil was short for Free Willy.

I was beginning to realise that the older you get, the harder it is to get fit. When I was young I could pretty much eat whatever I wanted, but ever since turning 35, I seemed to be putting on kilos in my sleep. And I knew it was only going to get

THE OLD AND THE BEAUTIFUL

worse. I was having visions of myself lying on the couch eating Pringles and watching *The Biggest Loser*, and then being lifted out of my house by a crane live on *Ricki Lake*. I even had a recurring nightmare in which *Today Tonight* was doing one of those hard-hitting reports into dodgy diets, and as they cut to the slow-mo stock footage of all the big beach bums bursting out of their budgie smugglers, I recognised my own arse.

I seemed to have stacked on a heap of weight in my face. You know it's time to cut the carbs when even Bert Newton looks at you and says, 'Gee, your head looks big!' Seriously folks, my noggin had become so enormous planets were orbiting around it. One night when I was asleep, NASA landed a rocket on my forehead, planted a flag on my nose, and claimed it in the name of the USA.

With my extra padding and humungous head, I looked like a football mascot. And it was definitely fat; the other day I picked a pimple and whipped cream and jam leaked out. (On the upside, due to my super-size face I was getting much better reception on my television; I was even offered a part-time job as a sightscreen at the next Ashes series.)

Anyway, I was as chubby as hell and I decided I wasn't going to take it anymore. Everyone told me the secret was diet and exercise. That's where my problem lay: my diet was awful and sadly, no matter how many fit people I've licked, I have never caught the exercise bug.

I really needed to shift those pounds, so I decided to embark on a serious fitness regimen. (It was either that or liposuction, a serious ice addiction, being incarcerated in Guantánamo Bay or eating in restaurants with unhygienic food preparation areas in the hope that I might get food poisoning.)

The first thing I did was join a gym.

Now, before I continue, I should point out that I've never been a gym junkie – which is a weird term now that I think about it. It conjures images of people standing outside Fitness First saying, 'Hey mate ... have you got fifty cents ... I just need a quick ten reps!'

In fact, the only time I'd attempted a gym work-out I woke up the next day so sore that even my eyelashes hurt, and I never went back. Plus, it always seemed stupid to pay money to pick up heavy things, when if there's something heavy at my house that needs to be picked up I pay someone else to do it.

So it was with some trepidation that I went to my first assessment session. Walking through the door of the amazing brand-new gym (I was already hoping that I wouldn't break anything really expensive), I spotted a massive boxing-ring (I half-expected Shannon Noll to be there and Ashton Kutcher to jump out and yell 'Punk'd!') and was introduced to the chiselled Adonis who was going to show me around. It didn't help my nerves that he looked me up and down and said, 'Hello, my name is Attila!'

Attila? Attila??? *Attila???* I introduced myself to the girl behind the counter half-expecting her to say her name was Genghis Khan. But as it turned out, Attila was an awesome bloke. He was a former triathlete who'd tried to design a gym that wasn't just exercise equipment, but included heaps of fun stuff like rock-climbing and boxing – and there was even a deejay!

(Although I did wonder if it would be a good gig. Imagine this exchange: 'Hey dude, where are you playing on the weekend? Do you have a session at a club, maybe the Boiler Room at the Big Day Out?' 'Nah mate, this week I'm on the wheels of steel down at the gym.' I guess in both places there are a lot of sweaty people drinking water.)

But I digress.

I filled in my forms – just doing the paperwork made me break out into a mild sweat – and then it was time to do some real exercise. After a little warm-up (and there I was thinking that's what the paperwork was for), first item on the agenda was, wait for it, pulling a car using a rope. At least I think that was one of the exercises. Either that or Attila needed a jumpstart and he was taking the piss.

From there we moved onto push-ups – I had to see how many I could do in a minute. While I admit I didn't make the entire minute without stopping, this should be no indication of my performance in the bedroom.

Then there were sit-ups (at least I made the minute this time), bench-press (normally the only thing I press into a bench is my fat arse), holding the medicine ball above my head while stepping through tyres (I'm sure that one is bound to come in handy next time I need to hold something heavy above my head while stepping through tyres) and chin-ups, which were really hard. There I was thinking it would be a piece of piss given all the chins I had on the go!

Next I got to swing on the monkey bars (I'm not sure if this was one of the exercises, or just recess; I was half-hoping for a game of down-ball or elastics). Then came a great one where Attila made me sprint up a set of steps, but take the escalator back down (the perfect time to sneak in a quick smoke).

Finally it was time to jump into the boxing ring to see how many punches I could throw in a minute. To be honest, by this stage my arms were trembling so much I struggled to put on the gloves in a minute; but luckily my manager Don King had paid off the judges, so I won by a nose.

At last, I was done. Sweaty, sore, stretched and broken, I resolved then and there to come back – the following year when my body had stopped aching.

The only other time I've been in that much pain was when I went on a skiing holiday with some uni mates. Growing up as humble dairy-farmers, my family didn't go on too many skiing trips. The only massive dumps I experienced in my childhood tended to come out of the rear end of cows. So when a couple of friends suggested we go to the snow for a week I leapt at the opportunity. Little did I know it would be the last time I was capable of leaping, or even walking, for the next month.

You see, I didn't realise that while some people see skiing as a wonderful way to spend a couple of weeks, I unfortunately suffer from a hereditary medical condition known as Uncoitis Completis (or in layman's terms, 'being a complete unco').

While my mates had a great time, over the next few days I spent so much of my time facedown in ice that I thought I was going to get drafted by the West Coast Eagles. And when I wasn't facedown, I was arse up. I think they made a mistake by attaching the skis to the bottom of my boots; they should have just attached them to my bottom, seeing as that was the part of my body that made the most contact with the snow. Seriously folks, by the end of the day my backside resembled Sylvester Stallone's face at the end of *Rocky*. My bum was so purple that when I bent over it looked like Dorothy the Dinosaur was trying to moon someone.

I also ended up with my ankles behind my ears so often it looked less like I was skiing and more like I was auditioning positions for a new and improved Kama Sutra. I spent so much time doing the splits even Britney Spears would've thought I looked a little trashy.

Foolishly, I'd hoped the trip might be an opportunity for romance, but the only legs that ended up wrapped around my back were my own. (Plus, at the end of a day on the slopes my body was so bruised and broken that the only person I wanted touching me was a licensed medical professional ... or possibly a coroner.)

All jokes aside, I returned from that trip convinced that skiing was invented by the same person who came up with colonics, circumcision and the Crazy Frog ring tone. It's entertainment for masochists while their dungeons are being cleaned during the winter. Sometimes I think the only thing separating a skiing holiday from a suicide pact is that on the skiing holiday there's a little more lycra and many more blokes called Hans.

I mean, if you need any evidence, just look at the equipment. You have to question any sport where they strap you into your footwear the same way they strap criminals into the electric chair on death row. I'm told that ski boots are so sturdy in order to give you plenty of ankle support, but to me they seem to be designed to snap your leg off at the knee when you fall over. (I often think they should improve efficiency by fitting your boots and crutches at the same time.)

Then there are the skis, which are made from materials like fibreglass and composite-laminated carbon fibre so they don't snap easily the way pesky things like, well, um, bones and ligaments do. They are also made of brightly coloured material, which makes them easy to find at the bottom of the mountain after you've fallen over and rescuers are trying to find and identify your body in the snow.

Not only were my skis colours that Ken Done would have thought were a bit loud, they also contained secret magnets at the end – try as I might to keep them straight, they would go in the complete opposite direction. Anthony Callea had more chance of going straight than I did.

Experienced skiers will tell you that the best way to slow down is something called a 'snow plough'. Unfortunately, my favoured method was running into something. Normally it was a tree or a rock, but if I was really lucky my fall was cushioned by another learner who was trying to do the snow plough.

As well as discovering that skiing is painful and dangerous, I also learned that it is ridiculously expensive. I secretly think skiing was invented by people who had too much money and just couldn't be bothered spending all day flushing it down the toilet. The slopes are full of rich people – like chiropractors and physiotherapists – who became wealthy fixing the many injuries people get on their skiing holidays.

If you want to get the same effect but save yourself some cash, here's what you need to do. Grab a mate, a plank of wood and a $2 bag of ice from the local service station. Then simply get your mate to bash you repeatedly with the wood and the ice for about an hour, and afterwards have a cup of hot Milo. That's pretty much what skiing is like.

So, neither skiing nor gym were going to help me in my battle against the bulge. Contemplating my options, I consulted my friends for some advice.

One of my hippie mates suggested yoga, but I thought it might be a bit much too soon since eating yoghurt was a little too healthy for me at this stage. Plus, I knew that no matter how hard I tried, I would never reach enlightenment while strangers were breaking wind right in front of me. (I'd been told that the moves in yoga were 'salute to the sun', 'downward dog' and 'pull my finger'.) As for Bikram yoga: if I really wanted to sweat, I'd just fly to Bali with a boogie-board bag filled with marijuana.

A fit female friend said she'd drag me along to her aerobics class, but as I'm known to get hot and sweaty sitting on the couch watching *Aerobics Oz Style* on the telly, I feared this might push me over the edge. And anyway, if it truly was 'Oz' style, surely there should have been fewer women doing star jumps in lycra and more blokes in stubbies and singlets doing arm curls with the remote control in one hand and a beer in the other?

Another mate tried to get me interested in cycling, which I concede is great for fitness and wonderful for the environment. But if there is one thing I enjoy less than exercise, it would have to be having my genitals worn away by a hard vinyl seat. Sure, I wanted to look better, but feeling like someone had taken an orbital sander to my nether regions wasn't exactly what I was after. I know you're meant to 'feel the burn', I just wanted to keep that sensation as far away from my pants as possible.

Which basically left me with jogging.

The day after my first jog I was stiffer than a bunch of teenage boys who'd just discovered their dad's secret stash of Viagra. But after much pain and perseverance, these days I actually quite enjoy it (even though the only sporting thing about me is the sports bra I need to hold my man boobs in place). After all, it's the only way I can hear heavy breathing without writing my mobile number on the Australian cricket team's dressing-room door.

But I'm hopeless at it. You know how on *Baywatch*, The Hoff used to run in slow-motion down the beach? Well, that's what I look like all the time. I am less a sprinter and more a shuffler, which is great if you're running the blackjack table at the casino but not if you're trying to lose some weight. I guess if you had to pick a piece of music to describe my jogging style, it would be less 'Wind Beneath My Wings' and more 'Running to Stand Still'.

The great thing is, I always feel like I'm exercising for another five minutes after I stop running, because that's how long it takes my man boobs to stop jiggling. I just have to remember not to make any calls on my mobile within ten minutes of finishing my jog, because with the amount of huffing and puffing I do, I run the risk of being arrested for obscene phone calls. Seriously, some days I walk up a set of stairs and start wheezing so hard Darth Vader offers me his asthma puffer.

I like to run near the harbour or seaside whenever I can – not to enjoy the awesome views, but because that's where most of those buskers pretending to be statues tend to congregate, and they're the only people I look fast next to.

And let's not even get into the oxymoron that is 'fun run'. It's the biggest lie since someone came up with the title of *Australia's Funniest Home Videos*.

I once considered entering a marathon, until I found out they expect you to run the whole 42 kilometres in a row. I was thinking I might spread it out over a couple of months.

The only reason I'd ever run a marathon is if there was a mugger behind me in a balaclava and running shorts, carrying a knife, chasing me the entire way. (Well, and maybe if there was free beer at every drink station, or Krispy Kremes at the end instead of water and oranges.)

Actually, now that I think about it, I have the perfect sport for me – sumo wrestling. You're allowed to eat what you want and, even though I might not lose any weight, standing next to those big boys will make me look good by comparison. You see (in case it isn't clear by now), I'm lazy and I love to eat. In fact, I think the only reason I got into entertainment is that when I am talking, it's the only time I can't shove food in my pie-hole.

Sometimes I think the best way for me to lose some weight would be to have someone break my jaw – so if you ever see me in a room with Shannon Noll, you'll know I'm about to start a diet. Although, that said, I'm the sort of guy who'd find a way to suck Pringles and pizza through a straw.

I've never been one for the food pyramid. My diet has always been more of a food bouncy castle, with the castle filled with cake and pudding and ice-cream and caramel sauce. It has always been thus. When I was a kid, I was not-so-little a kid. Put it this way, you know you should probably try a salad when the PE teacher gets the other kids to exercise by running laps around you. The only way he could convince *me* to run laps of the oval was to use a lure like they do at the greyhounds – instead of a rabbit, he had a bucket of KFC.

One day, upon waking up on the grass after a snooze at recess, I found that I had been declared a sacred site and Japanese tourists were climbing me.

Another time I came home from school with two black eyes. When my parents assumed I'd been in a fight with a bully, I didn't have the heart to tell them I'd been skipping and my boy boobs had hit me in the face. (While we're on the topic, as a former boombalada I have always thought that the current epidemic of childhood obesity can be linked to the crackdown on schoolyard bullying. Personally, I liked to think of the bullies more like angry personal trainers. When they stole my lunch money it meant I couldn't spend it on cake.)

But I digress. I was in Grade 6 when I realised I was desperately in need of an image makeover, a little *Queer Eye for the Who-Ate-All-the-Pies Guy*. The first step in my quest to make myself more popular was to score a cool new nickname. I decided on 'Donuts', partly because they're my favourite food, and I guess partly because I thought the other kids would Go Nuts For Donuts.

I had a cunning plan. I bought myself a giant box of donuts and at recess and lunchtime I'd stroll around eating them, like some sort of enigmatic tubby teenage Bond villain. My theory was, if people saw me eating donuts all the time, they'd think, 'Hey, that's the kid who eats donuts. You know what? We should call him . . . Donuts!' And a legend would be born. Foolproof, huh?

And it worked. Well, sort of. The other kids did start calling me something. Unfortunately it wasn't 'Donuts', it was 'Fatty Fatty Boombah' – but at least I had a nickname.

THREE

DOING IT FOR THE KIDS

I love kids, I really do. But I have to confess that I love them in the same way I love democracy or really dangerous roller-coaster rides: great idea in principle, but I certainly shouldn't be left in charge of them.

So I found myself a little out of my depth recently when I attended my nephew's first birthday party. I don't really attend a lot of parties for the pre-pre-pre-schooler set, especially since the restraining order stopped me from working as a children's clown.

The first thing I noticed when I rocked up to the party were the photos. There were so many pictures of my nephew Riley on the wall, it was treading a fine line between dedicated and loving and serial killer obession.

Then I noticed that I'd clearly misread the invitation. I thought it'd said, 'Please bring a plate', but it must have been, 'Please bring a baby.' Everyone at the party seemed to have at least one kid. And look, I don't want to sound baby-ist, but they all look pretty much the same to me. (As far as I'm concerned, all kids under the age of one look as if someone put Gandhi in the washing machine for too long.)

Suddenly I was very glad of the photo wall, because if I forgot which one was Riley, I could just pick up a baby, hold it against the wall and compare. Kind of like a tiny toddler line-up.

Being virtually the only non-breeder in the room, I couldn't participate in most of the discussions. At one stage, the topic was whether it's appropriate to let someone else breastfeed your child. Suddenly all eyes turned to me: 'Well, Wil? What do you think?'

What did I think? Aside from really needing another beer, I had to be honest and say I didn't know what I thought. No disrespect to mums, but for me breasts are still recreational. So, I just opened my mouth and said the first thing that came to mind: 'No, I don't think they should. I think babies should eat at home.'

At this stage I realised that instead of a beer, I had accidentally opened a can of worms. 'But what if your baby was crying?' I was asked.

'Well,' I said, 'it's my understanding that babies cry for a whole range of reasons: hunger, gas, tiredness, gas, teething, gas, the situation in the Middle East, gas, soiled nappies, gas – or simply seeing a repeat of the episode of *A Country Practice* when Molly dies. And anyway, if the crying is so bad, surely you can find something else to put in their mouth?'

'Yes,' one voice said, 'but what if they're hungry?'

I started to panic. I could feel the sweat dripping from my forehead, and blurted out, 'Well, as far as I can tell, most kids look a bit chubby; they could probably afford to miss a couple of meals, or at least try the occasional salad.'

At this point I knew I was in trouble. As if sensing blood, all eyes in the room turned towards me and the questions started to fly thick and fast: 'But surely it's just food, isn't it?'

'Technically, yes. But if that were completely true, could breastfeeding women go to the movies? Wouldn't that be considered bringing in outside food?' I replied.

'OK then, but what if I had your baby in the desert and breastmilk was the only food that could prevent starvation?'

I began to get an insight into what it might be like at Guantánamo Bay. I decided the best form of defence was offence. 'I guess the first question I'd ask is, what the hell are you doing with my baby in the desert? I mean, I know kids like making sandcastles, but try the beach first.'

'Yeah, fair point,' my inquisitor conceded, 'But how about this then: What if a plane crashed in the mountains and the only food left available to feed your child was my breastmilk?'

I knew I was beaten. At this point, I was just desperate

to keep a shred of dignity. 'OK, I give in. In that situation I would let you feed my baby. But – and this is a massive but – to me, this falls into the same category as cannibalism.'

I could tell I had the crowd hooked, so I continued. 'Yes, I would let my baby be fed breastmilk in that situation, just like I'd probably eat a human being to survive. But it doesn't mean I'm about to start eyeing up someone on a plane just because we've been sitting on the tarmac for fifteen minutes and they haven't brought around any peanuts.'

From the looks on people's faces, I doubted I'd be booked for babysitting jobs by the end of the afternoon.

However, from what I've seen at the local shopping mall recently, there isn't much to looking after kids these days – you just put them on a really tight leash. Now some of you may think I am talking metaphorically here: 'Yes, I brought up my son as though he was in the army from the age of seven.' But no, I mean literally. I'm referring to an actual leash. Do you know the ones I mean? I can't go to my local mall these days without seeing parents dragging their kids around in a bloody harness.

Now, before I start my usual half-thought-through ranting and raving, a slight disclaimer. As you know, I am not a parent, and if I was, the fear of losing one of my kids would terrify me. But I'm still pretty sure that I would never feel the need to put them on a leash.

I mean, what next? A collar with a bell and a name tag? Why stop there? If parents are so worried about their kids going missing, why don't they take them down to the local vet and get them microchipped?

I'm sorry, but every time I see a kid in a harness it makes me feel uncomfortable. Surely a child is not a dog, despite how tempting it must be, when they go to the toilet on the carpet, to grab them and rub their nose in it. For me, the leash is one step too far.

How do parents exercise their kids these days? Do they take them to the park, throw a stick and get them to fetch? (Or will they be too busy sniffing the other kids' bums?) It's only a small step to tying the kid to a pole out the front of the shops while they duck in to grab the newspaper. When the kid is crying too loud, just put him in the backyard with a squeaky toy and a bone.

Again, I stress that I am not a parent, but if I should find myself playing that role one day, I hope I'll be able to teach my kid boundaries and not simply tie them to a rope to keep them within a three-metre radius.

I mean, if parents are so worried about letting their kids out of their sight, why bother even cutting the umbilical cord in the first place? That way, they'll never get too far away, and for fun Mum can bounce them up and down like a yoyo.

In fact, maybe it's time we considered bringing in a parenthood test before we let people breed. It sounds like an outrageous idea, but think about it: we have a citizenship test now, and who do you reckon is the bigger threat to the future of Australian society: dodgy immigrants or dickhead dads?

It's always struck me as slightly absurd that if you want to go fishing in this country you need a licence, but anyone can have a baby. Surely something's slightly out of whack when you have to pass a higher standard to dangle a rod in water than you do to dangle your rod in . . . well, you get what I mean.

There's no doubt in my mind that being a parent is the hardest job in the world. Maybe we should have higher standards. Everyone accepts without question that you have to pass a test to drive a car, but any idiot can do the most important job of all – raise another human being.

Maybe it is time we introduced a 'Licence to Breed' (although it does sound a bit like a dodgy James Bond sequel). It could be similar to the driver's licence – if you wanted to have a baby you'd first have to wait until you were sixteen, and then have two years on your L-plates. But this wouldn't mean you could only 'practise' making a baby with your mum there telling you what to do.

Then, once you got to eighteen and passed your Licence to Breed you'd be able to start making babies. But like your driver's licence, not if you had been drinking heavily. And they could implement a series of demerit points. Smoking while pregnant: lose three points; naming your child after a celebrity's baby: lose three points; knitting your kid a footy jumper when everyone else gets one from the shop: lose six points.

Oh, and if a cop pulls you over while you have your kid on a leash, instant suspension of licence.

DOING IT FOR THE KIDS

While we're on the topic of demonising mums, why did Madonna cop such flak over her adoption of a little boy from Malawi? I mean, Michael Jackson, yeah, but Madonna? Surely if she was giving a kid the chance to be like an orphan, adopted for the very first time, then it had to be a good thing? If it works out badly, at least Britney's kids will have someone to carpool with to therapy sessions.

Don't get me wrong. I understand how hard it must be for couples who've been going through the painful process of adoption – sometimes for years. But the way the media portrayed it, you'd think Madge had been sitting outside kindergartens snatching babies from prams with her teeth. Forget the dingo, think, 'My baby! Madonna took my baby!'

OK, yes, some feared that Madonna was only adopting as a fashion statement – not helped when she asked if they had any kids with red hair, because it would match the furniture better. But if she sparks a trend of interest in African orphans, it can only be positive. (And it could have been worse. She could have ordered a kid on eBay. Or should that be eBaby?) Let's be honest, before this, most people thought Malawi was the name of one of Bob Geldof's children.

Anyway, Madonna angrily denied that she was simply following the latest fad; and if you don't believe her, ask her yoga guru, feng shui expert and kabbalah adviser. She was even on *Oprah* – well, not *on* Oprah, that would have been a whole new scandal – defending herself, saying she didn't expect all the controversy. In fact, she asked the press to leave her alone so she could get back to her quiet, boring life of crucifying herself on stage in front of thousands of people, just like any regular mother.

There are plenty of reasons you could get mad at Madonna – especially if she announced plans to make *Swept Away 2: The Sandy Crack is Back* – but is taking a kid from a life of poverty to a life of luxury really her biggest crime? We have to remember that these kids live in a country where there are millions of orphans. If Madonna hadn't come along, the next plan was to start a rumour they were at risk of being eaten by cannibals in the hope of getting Naomi Robson to adopt them.

Yes, I appreciate the argument about keeping kids in their own culture, but if you live in a country where the average wage is a dollar a day, being adopted by Madonna would be like winning the lottery. (When he heard that Madonna was adopting babies, even 'Baby John' Burgess put up his hand.)

I reckon if you asked most Malawian kids what they wanted to do when they grow up, they'd probably say, 'To be adopted by Angelina Jolie or Madonna. Hey, I'd even settle for Dannii Minogue . . . as long as she doesn't sing me to sleep.' So before you rush to condemn Madonna, pause for a minute. These kids live in a country where the life expectancy is thirty-seven years. When I hear that, all I can think is how lucky we are. In Oz, that's not even old enough to start contemplating your midlife crisis. I have mates who hadn't even finished their degrees by thirty-seven. Now, instead of wondering where his next meal is coming from, little David will have all the food he needs. Admittedly, it's English food, but beggars can't be choosers.

That said, there are some downsides to having the Material Girl as your mum. For starters, you can't be breastfed, because that conical bra of hers will take your eye out. Plus, the first person most kids see naked is their mother, but David is the only person in the world who hasn't seen Madonna without her kit on. And finally, there's the problem with his name. He's the child of a celebrity now; surely it can't be long before Madge changes his name by deed-poll to Strawberry-Jam-Trousers?

But at the end of the day, it seems to me that people have been just a tad bad to Mads, and it makes me sad. After all, she's not only given someone a new life and the chance to meet Elton John, she's reportedly donated $5 million to programs that support Malawian orphans.

Maybe she did put the Mad in Madonna by buying little David a $12,300 rocking horse when the money would have been better spent at the local Malawi Sizzler, but when all is said and done, I'm sure she loves each one of her kids very much and David will have a wonderful life.

In fact, Madge, if you ever want a thirty-five-year-old stand-up comic with man boobs as a son, I'm available. To some that may sound far-fetched, but Madonna clearly has a bit of a fetish for adoption: why not me too? According to reliable sources, one of the reasons her marriage to Guy

Ritchie went belly-up is because Guy couldn't relate to his wife's 'fascination with adopting children'. Madge, I know where you're coming from. In fact, one of the questions that's been worrying me of late is, how many cats is too many?

Seriously folks, at what point do you go from ordinary mild-mannered pet owner to the feature story on *A Current Affair*? (You know, the one they wedge between 'When Good Washing Machine Repairmen Go Bad' and their hard-hitting exclusive on how nine out of ten people with taste-buds can actually believe that 'I Can't Believe It's Not Butter' is not butter.) At what point do you cross the line? Is it when you have more than two? More than ten? When you start knitting your kittens their own clothes? Is it when you give up and replace all the carpet in your house with old newspapers, or when all your cats have their own MySpace pages? When do you go from committed animal-lover to Crazy Old Cat Lady who should be committed?

The reason I pose this doozy is that Amy and I have just adopted our third kitten — I think he realises we're not his real parents — and we're a little worried that if we take in too many more animals, the neighbours will think we're building an ark in the backyard.

Some of our friends have cruelly suggested that our cats are nothing more than substitute babies, but I don't think this is true. For starters, I'm pretty sure that if you went to dinner and a movie and left your baby locked in the house for five hours with nothing more than a bowl of water and a tray of sand for them to crap in, the authorities would get involved. (And if you're breastfeeding your kitten, you probably should talk to someone – like a producer from *The Jerry Springer Show*.)

Now, before I go any further, I should deal with the whole 'men and cats' issue. For some reason, in this country if a man says, 'I like cats', what people actually hear is, 'I have my period, now get me a hot-water bottle and a block of chocolate because I want to watch *Grey's Anatomy*.' Put it this way, there is no line in the VB ad that says, 'You can get it stroking your cat's tummy until he goes meow; matter of fact, I've got it now!'

Don't get me wrong, I love dogs too. When you get home a dog is so happy to see you they will meet you at the door, lick your face for an hour, and then try to make puppies with your leg. Forget going whacko for Shmackos, I think the minute you go out of the house most dogs are smoking ice. (If I ever did get a dog, it would be a sniffer dog. At the very least they'd be great fun to take to parties.)

Dogs are great. But dogs are easy. A cat, on the other hand, will simply glance up from their armchair when you get home from work, put down their catnip martini and cigar, and look at you as if to say, 'Oh, you've been out, have you? I didn't notice . . . now get me some food!' If a cat loves you, you feel you've earned that love.

Basically, the difference between cats and dogs is that while you own a dog, the cat owns you. If you throw a stick for a dog, the dog will go and fetch the stick, bring it back and be happy for you to throw it again. If you dared throw a stick for a cat, the cat would look at you as if to say, 'Wow, I guess you really didn't want that stick ... now get me some food!'

Sure, there are some downsides to owning a kitten. You can buy them all the fancy toys and scratching posts in the world, but there'll be nothing they enjoy more than destroying something really valuable and irreplaceable. And then there's the scratching. And by that I don't mean that our cat bought a couple of decks and started deejaying under the name 'Snoop Catty Cat'. I love our new kitten, but my arms currently have so many scars that I look like a thirty-five-year-old emo.

Oh, and obviously I don't approve of the way they bring in little lizards from the garden as presents. For starters, it's obviously wrong that they kill native wildlife; and secondly, if they really want to get me a present, screw the lizard, how about an iPod, or at least an offer to dry-clean the $400 coat they've been using as a bed.

But the upsides far outweigh the downsides. Even scientifically. For example, there are demonstrated links between kids who are violent to animals and adults who are violent to humans. So, if you want to stop your kids from being violent, get them a pet and teach them to treat it with respect and kindness. Or as the bumper stickers I'm printing will put it: 'Get Your Kid a Cat and They Won't Be Ivan Milat!'

I'm grateful to my folks for letting me have pets as a kid,

but I'm still upset I never got to celebrate Halloween. I was so jealous of American kids getting to go trick or treating. Sadly, where I grew up, if someone you didn't know offered you lollies, it was usually time to involve the authorities. (Apparently in the States, parents tell their kids, 'Don't take candy from strangers ... unless you are dressed as Dracula, then it's OK.')

As a child I was fascinated by the idea that once a year it was totally acceptable — nay, *encouraged* — to go from door to door dressed as Spiderman and ask people you didn't know for chocolate.

Ah, who am I kidding? Even as an adult I think it's awesome. I love the idea of going to someone's house and scaring them into giving you free stuff. However, I should pause here for a moment to point out that when you do this as a kid, it's really cute. When you try the same thing as an adult, for some reason people don't find it as charming, and instead of calling it 'trick or treating', the judge refers to it as 'aggravated breaking and entering'. (Although now that I think about it, Halloween would be the perfect opportunity for dwarf burglars, or midgets with the munchies.)

But I digress.

When I was about eight or nine I remember feeling really ripped off that I'd been born in Australia, where, if you went around asking people for food, it was called begging. 'Please sir ... can I have some more ... Skittles?' I was as mad as Halloween and I wasn't going to take it anymore. Why was

I being denied my god-given (or in this case pagan-given) rights?

I wanted to dress up as Dracula. I wanted to bob for apples, or give apples to Bob, or whatever you were meant to do. (Although why Bob would want apples when there were free lollies was beyond me.) I wanted to eat chocolate until I sweated nougat, and carve faces into pumpkins and light candles inside them so it looked like Bert Newton was staring out my front window. (In retrospect, seeing I was quite a chubby kid – I think the technical term is boombalada – I probably would have been better off eating the pumpkin and setting fire to the chocolates.)

And I guess, in these days of childhood obesity, the last thing we need is to encourage kids to go doorknocking for lollies. On the upside, the walk would probably do them good. Maybe we could even take it a step further? 'Yes, you can have a fun-sized Mars Bar. But first you have to drop and give me twenty!'

Anyhoo, where was I? Oh, that's right, Halloween. Now, don't get me wrong: as an adult any area in which we don't slavishly copy the Americans is a ray of sunshine. Yo, you know what I'm saying, dude? Fo shizzle. Holla if you hear me beeyatch.

And even though it's getting harder to tell them apart, I'm glad Aussie kids are still different from the Yanks. Let's face it, these days in the States, the main reason people give treats to kids standing at their door is not because it's Halloween – it's because they're holding Uzis.

Even so, the big, pimply, nougat-sweating kid inside me is still slightly disappointed that we don't open the all-you-can-eat trick or treat Halloween buffet. It's also why a couple of years ago, on the evening of 31 October, the knock at my door came as a complete shock to me.

It was even more of a shock when I was greeted by a witch and a vampire. Now, either the Mormons were having a *Buffy the Vampire Slayer* theme night, or I was being trick-or-treated. Turns out it was a couple of kids, aged five and six, who'd just moved to Australia from the USA and didn't want to miss Halloween. (I should point out that this information was conveyed by their dad, who was standing behind them. They hadn't just flown to Australia by themselves on some elaborate chocolate scam.)

Anyway, as they held out the pillowcases they were using as lolly bags – and yes, I did just snigger when I wrote 'lolly bag' – and proclaimed 'trick or treat', I started to panic. You see, I knew for certain there was no chocolate in the house. I knew this, because I'd eaten it all about half an hour earlier. Indeed, in the last five minutes I'd resorted to eating Milo out of the can with a spoon to get a choccie fix. What could I give them?

I knew there was some dried fruit and nuts in the cupboard, but the fat kid inside me also realised what a crap treat that would be. It's trick or treat, not trick or healthy-snack-that-will-also-make-you-regular. I rushed to the fridge, but since it was a bachelor pad this was no help at all. All I had was a six-pack of beer and some assorted condiments. I briefly considered giving them the booze, but figured that witches should be more concerned with eye of newt than getting as pissed as a newt. And the unopened jar of marinated garlic seemed equally inappropriate, given that one of the kids was dressed as a vampire.

I looked at their hopeful faces and my heart broke. So I ransacked the flat and grabbed whatever I could find. The witch and vampire ended up leaving with their pillowcases stuffed with six CDs, a digital alarm clock and a $30 JB Hi-Fi voucher I'd got for my birthday.

❋ ❋ ❋

Speaking of little kids, on a recent flight, I found myself seated next to a six-year-old boy called Josh. He was a cute kid, with a big mop of curly hair, kind of how Dicky Knee would look if he were brought to life Pinocchio-style.

I don't usually like to sit next to kids on planes. Now, I'm not saying that six-year-old boys don't have their place, but it's normally performing in *Billy Elliot* or using their nimble fingers to make cheap sneakers in sweatshops. I really like kids, I do, but it's sad that in this day and age you feel uncomfortable as an adult man talking to a six-year-old. Like if you do it for too long either the authorities are going to get involved or Gary Glitter will ask you to join his Facebook group.

Anyway, no sooner had we taken off than Josh started bitching that he wasn't in business class, where his parents were. 'You know what I like about business class?' he said. 'The leg room.'

The kid was six. Not six-foot-six. Six years old. And he liked business class for the leg room? His legs didn't even touch the floor in economy! He could have lain down comfortably in the overhead compartment!

Anyway, here's what I learned from Josh:

Fact: *Smoking can kill you, but so can rugby.* Well, that's true; and, if you smoke a lot you tend to smell like you've had your head up another man's bum, much like rugby.

Fact: *It would be really cool if you had a tunnel in your house that could take you anywhere you wanted to go in the entire world.* Yes, that would be cool, but I think they'd still come up with some way to lose your luggage.

Fact: *Tractors would be much cooler if they could do backflips.* That is a fact. There's no way you can argue with that. And it would also mean we'd see a lot more farmers finally getting involved in the *Crusty Demons of Dirt*.

Fact: *You can get cancer from smoking, even if you eat vegetables.* And the risk might be increased if you smoked the vegetables. Also, I think you can still get hurt playing rugby if you eat vegetables.

Fact: *A kid my class once filled his mouth with water, then spat it on his pants and told everyone he'd done a wee. It was hilarious.* You see, that's another area where water restrictions have hurt society: now you can only do that prank on Wednesday and Sunday after six.

Fact: *Bats weigh a kilo, except for Batman who weighs more than that.* Yes, but you'd hardly know it, because that black outfit is very slimming.

Fact: *Sprite and lemonade are the same thing, they just come in different cans.* Hang on, next he'll be telling me that most people can't tell the difference between Coke and Pepsi, *Today Tonight* and *A Current Affair*, or any of the various Daddos.

Fact: *The cans of drink you get on a plane don't fit a lot of drink in them, but if the cans were as long as the plane, they would really fill you up, but you wouldn't be able to fit them on the plane.* Well, you can't argue with that . . .

(I should probably point out that these last two facts were prompted by the arrival of the flight attendant offering us drinks. I thought it was great that Josh had facts for all occasions.)

Fact: *I once got dirt in my teeth, but it's OK, I didn't die.* I was glad to hear this, and I suddenly realised I might have been having a Bruce Willis moment. I was also glad he didn't die of 'dirt teeth'; it has already taken so many of our young ones, and yet nobody has given it a benefit concert or even a ribbon.

Fact: *A boy in my class once picked his nose and ate it.* Personally, I think there's probably more chance you'd die of that than dirt in your teeth.

Fact: *Your house would be cooler if it had wings and could fly places and you wouldn't need to stay in hotels.* Although it'd probably be a bitch trying to get a parking space; and have you ever tried to reverse-park a house?

Fact: *I know the s-word, the f-word and the other s-word.* When I asked what the other s-word was, he just looked at me and said, 'Shut-up!' For a moment I was taken aback; after all, in my day, young kids were taught to *never* swear in front of adults.

But no sooner had the thought entered my mind than I realised something quite profound: the moment you go from being young and cool to being an old codger is not related to age. It's when you start using the expression 'in my day'.

This is especially true when you combine 'in my day' with any of the following: 'People had manners', 'Children knew the real value of money', 'We wore our trousers around our waists not our knees' and 'Music was actually music, not this noise!'

I'm loath to admit that I've been dishing out 'in my day' way too frequently of late, so I guess it's only a matter of time before I'm wearing my pants around my nipples.

I find I'm particularly fuddy and/or duddy when it comes to matters of technology, such as digital cameras. While intellectually I understand the various advantages of digital technology, I still think it's kind of sad that kids today will never know what it's like to take photos and then have to wait five agonising days to find out whether in every shot the people's eyes are half-shut, as though at the exact moment the photographer said 'cheese' they had a stroke. (Let's face it, with digital cameras so prevalent, the only time you see bad photos of yourself are in passports and mug-shots.)

When I was young, picking up your photos from the chemist was like a lottery. Today's generation will never know what it feels like to get a whole roll of shots back only to discover your snap of the Eiffel Tower at sunset was completely obscured by your thumb.

They'll never know what it's like to have to urgently finish off a film, and thus end up with more photos of the pharmacist in their photo album than of members of their immediate family.

Sometimes it seems to me that technology has changed the entire purpose of taking photos. When I was young, photos acted as reminders of times past. These days, though, people will snap off a dozen photos and then examine them straightaway. 'Hey, do you remember this . . . and this?' Well, of course I do, it was only thirty seconds ago and I was there. In fact, I'm still here. That photo would only be useful if I suddenly suffered serious brain trauma or became a goldfish or Ozzy Osbourne.

And don't even get me started on the people who take so many photos that you could print them off, make a flip book and recreate the whole night.

Here's another one: in my day, people used to write letters. These days, kids seem to think 'letters' is the bit of the Big Mac that's left over once the two all-beef patties, cheese, pickles, onions and sesame seed bun have been eaten. (And the only stamps they're collecting are from nightclubs where they listen to their fancy doof music . . . well, *they* call it music! Oops, there I go again.) You know that nobody writes letters anymore when even your World Vision sponsor child sends you email or tells you to access their Facebook page.

Don't get me wrong, I like email, but it's nowhere near as good as an old-fashioned letter. A love email will never be as romantic as a love letter, no matter how many smiley-face emoticons you attach to the end. Plus, when you send an email you don't get to lick the back of the Queen; and if you get stuck on a deserted island, it's a whole lot harder to stick an email in a bottle. (Well, unless the island is equipped with a computer and a printer, in which case you're probably on Hamilton Island.)

And let's not forget that it's much less likely your regular mailbox will be filled with deals for cheap Viagra and offers to upsize your Junior Burger to a Big Mac, because people have to pay fifty-five cents every time they send a letter

Then there are mobile phones, which are now so ubiquitous that I think I saw an Amish talking on one the other day. (His ring tone was the theme from *Witness*.) My main gripe with mobile phones is they've made everything too convenient. Imagine how much less trouble Shane Warne would have found himself in if every time he felt in the mood he had to locate the nearest public phone box? (Only to discover that someone had cut the cord or jammed the slot with chewing gum.)

They've also completely destroyed the possibility of sharing exciting news with your partner at the end of the day. Before mobiles, you could come home and regale anyone who would listen with stories. Now it's more like, 'Did anything exciting happen at work today?' And you have to say, 'Well, you know it did! Remember I helped that woman give birth on the street? Remember I called you while she was having contractions, and then I sent you photos of the head crowning, and then you live-streamed the rest of the birth before I put the baby on to say hello?' (Actually, I'm talking up how exciting my life is. The truth is, it's more likely to be, 'Well, you know it did! I found that M&M that looks like the Dalai Lama . . . remember I sent you the photo?')

And don't even get me started on the fact that when I was a kid, if you wanted to take a photo, send an email, listen to music and make a phone call you actually needed a camera, a computer, a stereo and a telephone. These days, you can do it all from your mobile. I'll tell you one thing, it wouldn't have happened in my day.

Now, I'm not technophobic. I think people should be able to use technology as much as they like, in their own homes. Hey, some of my best friends are tech heads. In fact, it was those same friends who dragged me kicking and screaming into the 21st century – and I have to say, not a moment too soon. Put it this way, when I first heard that a computer had beaten the world's best chess player, I didn't marvel at the technology. My first thought was, 'Well, why don't we challenge the smart-arse computer to something we can win, like rugby league?'

In a relatively short space of time I have metamorphosed from a complete Luddite – even the Amish were sending me scornful emails from their wooden computers – to someone who is a total sucker for any new doodad (it's a technical term) on the market. My favourite gadget by far has to be my iPod. iPod therefore I am. I love it, yet I have to confess the feeling wasn't always mutual.

I got my first iPod back in the early days, when they were made of wood and you had to pedal a bike to get them to play more than two songs in a row. The main problem way back in YOT (Ye Olde Times) was that even though the technology enabled you to listen to thousands of songs in a row, the battery had a shorter life than most new Australian comedies on the Seven Network. You could theoretically play days worth of music, but the battery died so quickly the only way you could take it for a decent jog was if you had a really, really, really long extension cord.

Still, it was certainly an improvement on the discman, which, if you tried to take it jogging, made your *Best of Kamahl* sound like it had been remixed by Fatboy Slim. (Personally, I preferred the *really* good old days, when 'portable music' meant walking down the street with a giant ghetto-blaster on your shoulder. Then again, as you know I'm old skool; foshizzle my nizzle ... I'm also so white, albinos mock me.)

Anyhoo, my patience was rewarded as technology improved at a rapid rate – almost too rapid. Owning an iPod is kind of like being married to Rod Stewart: you know that in a couple of weeks a newer model is going to come along. In the shop they're the latest in cutting-edge technology, but by the time you get them home they're the equivalent of a puffy jacket, a 'Frankie Says Relax' T-shirt and Hammer pants. The 20GB iPod was followed by the 40GB colour iPod, then the 80GB video iPod with wings and a twist of lemon. I kept thinking, if I just hold off, soon they'll bring out the 160GB 3-D iPod, which makes you feel as if you're hanging out in a spa with the band. Although, if that were the case, I'd probably listen to a lot less Rolling Stones and a lot more Veronicas and Hi-5.

These days, there's an iPod that can hold 20,000 average-length songs – or the equivalent of about three Meatloaf albums. You do have to ask the question: who needs an iPod that can hold 20,000 songs? People who want to go for a jog . . . for the next eight years? Or people who need a compilation tape for their road-trip . . . to the moon? (Strangely, in the last year, the trend seems to be to make them smaller again. They have the Shuffle, the Nano, and soon the biPod – yes folks, it holds just two songs. Less than most cassingles!)

So why have iPods been so successful? Well, I think the main appeal of the pod is that everyone feels like they own their own radio station – if this trend continues, don't be surprised if people with iPods start approaching you on the street offering you 'icy-cold cans of Coke' or demanding that you identify the 'secret sound'.

Admittedly, iPods can be a pain for the person sitting next to the wearer on public transport. Sometimes I suspect there's a fault in the headphone design, because they seem louder to the outside world than they are to the wearer.

I love my iPod, but I don't embrace every innovation. For example, I don't get downloading movies to your iPod: 'Wow, *The Lord of the Rings* is visually spectacular ... what do you mean this is actually *Dirty Dancing*?' After all, most people have flat-screens in their houses that would make the MCG scoreboard feel like a man who's just emerged from a cold swimming pool next to Matt Shirvington. Most of them look less like TVs and more like U2 is about to pop around for an impromptu gig. And yet we're expected to watch shows on something so small you think you're watching Naomi Robson on *Today Tonight* but it's actually an old episode of *Mister Ed*.

And isn't it time we called a halt to all the various iPod accessories? First it was the novelty cover, then the speakers and the car set. The other day I even saw a plastic fish that dances when connected to the player. You know what? If you think a plastic fish is a good idea, then what you really need is a hobby. That is not something you need — that's a test to see if you have too much money! If you ever find yourself reaching for your credit card to buy a fish that dances when your iPod plays, give yourself a stiff uppercut, take the money and send it to a starving child in Africa – so they can buy a dancing fish and eat it.

Seriously folks, I'm all for technological advancement, but for me the justifying principle is that the new doodad must enhance your life in some way, and perhaps even improve you as a person. For example, I reckon I'm a much friendlier bloke since I got my new iPhone. But before I explain why, a little background.

Despite my best efforts – and I do try – I'm hopeless with names. I'm so bad I sometimes have to check the inside of my underpants just to remember who *I* am. For some reason, my brain has an uncanny capacity for retaining useless trivia, but anything important like names, birthdates, tax file numbers, car rego or my PIN gets erased like an Etch A Sketch every time I nod or sneeze. (I've lived in the same place for nearly three years and I still don't know my home phone number. Although, given I live alone, I don't know why I'd ever need to call my own house – unless I was asking the cats to tape *Survivor*.)

But I digress.

I find it amazing – and completely frustrating – that I can still clearly remember that Mrs Mangel caught the bouquet at Scott and Charlene's wedding on *Neighbours*, but often I'll be halfway through a conversation with someone I know and have to say, 'Excuse me, I'm so sorry, but what's your name again?' Only to have them stare at me, slowly shake their head, sigh and say, 'It's Graeme. But to be honest, normally you just call me Dad.'

I long for ye golden olden days when people were named after their jobs. That made life simple. The butcher was called Butcher, the baker was called Baker – though it does make you wonder what Steve Hooker's relatives did for a living. And come to think of it, I'm not a hundred percent sure how I'd feel about being called Wil Knob Gags.

The worst thing is, it's not as though I don't try to remember names. I've used every trick and technique, but they just seem to make it worse. For instance, someone suggested to me once that if you can't remember someone's name you should just ask them, 'So, how do you spell your name again?' The first time I tried this, the person I was talking to just stared at me and said, 'R . . . O . . . B!' Trying to save face I said, 'No, silly, I meant your last name', to which he replied, 'J . . . O . . . N . . . E . . . S!' At this point I decided to quickly change the topic by asking if he knew who'd caught the bouquet at Scott and Charlene's wedding on *Neighbours*.

Another favoured technique is to associate a person's name with a picture in your mind. When I tried this on my friend Rob, the only image I could think of was a robbery, and the next time I saw him I ended up dobbing him in to Crime Stoppers.

Another bit of advice I read on the internet was to take a couple of really deep breaths every time you meet someone new, because apparently when you're stressed the brain activates an enzyme that impairs short-term memory. Unfortunately, when I tried this everyone either thought I was having an asthma attack or was some sort of pervert. (Although it does raise the possibility that Darth Vader wasn't a heavy-breather after all; maybe he was just trying to remember all the stormtroopers' names.)

Something else I tried was repeating the person's name in conversation when I first met them, but that just made me sound like I was channelling *Rain Man*.

I tried looking directly into people's eyes when I met them, but for some reason when I do that my eyes can't focus, so not only did people think I was autistic, they also thought I was cross-eyed.

I even tried imagining their names written on their foreheads, but to be honest this would have been more effective if I'd simply grabbed a biro and written their names there for real.

Whatever the technique, I tried it, and it didn't work. I was ready to give up and resign myself to a life of constantly being embarrassed in social situations, until a little bit of technology changed my life forever. (I finally come to the point of my story; thanks for your indulgence.)

It all happened when I was invited to a function and had to confront what is basically my worst nightmare: a room full of people who were 'friends of a friend'. You know, the sort of people you've met once or twice so you *should* know their names, but you'd actually struggle to identify them in a line-up. (For some reason I would definitely point out my friend Rob in a line-up; there's just something about that dude that makes me suspicious.)

Then I had a sudden realisation. On my new iPhone I can access the internet. I quickly ducked into the toilets and looked up my mate's Facebook page, where there were photos of everyone at the party, with their names underneath. And not just their names. I strolled back into the party filled with confidence and conversation-starters: 'So, Jack, good to see you. Are you still into . . . Powderfinger? And Sally, it's good to see you, too. I was sad to hear you and Rob have gone from being 'in a relationship' to 'it's complicated'; but I've got to be honest, there was always something I didn't trust about that bloke.'

So, as you can see, I am well-sold on the idea that technology can be life-improving and worthwhile. However, I need to point out that my relationship with the gadgets in my life is far from smooth. My computer and I have a particularly tempestuous liaison.

The other day, for instance, no matter what I tried, I just couldn't turn it on. And no, I didn't spend the day dressed in sexy lingerie, saying 'hard drive' and 'RAM' in a husky voice. No, what I mean is, my computer just stopped working and I didn't know why. Perhaps it was some computer public holiday that I didn't know about. Was it the Bill Gates birthday long weekend?

Forget 'computer says no', I was ready to settle for my computer saying anything at all. It was as though my laptop had finally got sick of all the websites I made it look up and decided to give me the silent treatment.

Where was that freaking smug Microsoft paperclip when I really needed him? (I tried asking a regular paperclip for help, but people started staring at me weirdly and removing all the sharp items from my desk.) Is there anything worse than being greeted by a completely blank screen? Well, maybe watching the latest episode of Channel Ten's *The Wedge*.

To add insult to injury, I hadn't backed up my work. (To be honest, the only time I back up is if I eat too much cheese.) Of course, I should have known better. My computer goes down on me so regularly I have nicknamed it Paris.

The truth is, although I'm a convert to the technological revolution, it's never come easy to me. In fact, as my techie friends will tell you, when I got my first laptop, I thought it would only work if I shoved a five-dollar note in its disk drive every ten minutes. You know that book *Computers for Dummies*? Well, in the centrefold picture the Dummy is wearing an 'I'm With Stupid' T-shirt and it's pointing at me.

During that first tumultuous year of getting to know my new computer, whenever someone asked me to send a PDF to their Blackberry, I somehow ended up giving an STD to one of the Bananas in Pyjamas. The first time a friend said they'd googled me, I asked if I'd enjoyed it and whether they'd used protection.

Until a few years ago, the only broadband I'd ever heard of was the one that held up my trackie-daks. And when I got my first iPod, I had no idea how to get the songs

DOING IT FOR THE KIDS

onto my computer. I tried rubbing the CDs against the Apple, but that didn't seem to help. Yes, I'm ashamed to say that while most six-year-olds in countries where they don't have electricity can load songs onto an iPod, to me it was like watching David Copperfield and Gandalf teach Harry Potter magic tricks. It probably didn't help that most of my albums were on vinyl, and no matter how hard you try you simply can't fit a record in a computer's disk drive.

Anyway, back to my current crisis. Not only am I an *idiot savant* without the *savant*, when something does go wrong, I go to pieces. It's like I have the reverse Midas touch: everything I touch turns to crap. I'm always afraid I'll press Control-Alt-Delete and somehow erase the entire internet.

So, in order to get my computer working, I decided to carefully push the on button. (I hope I'm not getting too technical here; I know some of you must be thinking, 'Hey, slow down there egg-head.') But that didn't work, so I resolved to carefully push the on button again. This time I pushed harder – you know, in case the computer didn't hear me properly the first time. Yes, I was working on the same theory as most American tourists in non-English-speaking countries: if the people don't understand you the first time, just talk louder. Eventually, after numerous attempts without a response, I decided to give up on my computer and picked up a pen instead.

Now, this may sound extreme, but another piece of technology I'm ready to ditch is my car. I think it would be much more straightforward to trot around Sydney in a horse and cart, just as they did in the good ole days.

You see, I'm beginning to think my car is cursed. For starters, there's the smell. About six months ago, for no discernable reason, my car just started to stink. And I don't mean just a little bit. I'm talking about a smell that would make a bad smell hold its nose, a stench that would bring tears to an onion's eye.

You know how they talk about a stink so bad it could peel wallpaper? Well, this one could knock down entire walls. A dead body in the boot would actually make my car smell better rather than worse. It's as though every night a wet dog breaks into my car and uses it to mature unpasteurised blue cheese. It smells so bad that the other day I held a used pair of running socks to my nose to block out the odour. In fact, I secretly suspect that Michael Jackson's nose fell off immediately after catching a whiff of my vehicle as I drove by.

You know there's something seriously wrong when the dreadlocked backpacker who's just washed your windscreen leans into the window for his change and says, 'Dude, you should buy some air-freshener!' (By the way, I did try using one of those air-fresheners you hang from your rear-view mirror, but it just made the car smell like the wet dog had spent the night eating Mentos.)

With a smell that bad, my only option was to drive around with the windows open – which was when my second problem reared its ugly head.

You see, my automatic driver-side window has now decided that while it is happy to open, it won't close again unless I push the button while physically pulling up the glass with my other hand (and then pulling out my fingers at the last moment to ensure I don't sever my fingers in the process). For most people, the biggest fear when driving a car is having an accident. For me, it's never being able to juggle again. And I do have to get the window as high as possible, because my car has already been broken into.

Anyway, apart from the guillotine window and the sickly stench, things had been fine for a while – until everything fell apart.

First, my car was broken into. Then I got a flat tyre, only to discover when I went to grab the jack that the thieves had stolen that, too. I mean, seriously folks, who steals a jack? I've heard of a carjacking, but a car-jack jacking? Or maybe their getaway vehicle had a flat and they had to improvise? Is there a lucrative black jack market?

As if that weren't bad enough, the other morning I got into the car, turned the key, and it didn't work at all. I turned the key again. Still nothing. Turns out my battery had died (probably from the smell). Luckily, roadside assistance was quickly on the spot and replaced it with a new one. Only problem was, when I started the car again, I couldn't get the stereo to work.

Obviously my car has some sort of security override that means when the battery dies the stereo locks. Now, instead of belting out some nonstop blocks of rock, it was flashing 'Enter Code' in a way that implied if I didn't enter said code my car would self-destruct in thirty seconds.

But what code was I meant to enter? I tried the PIN for my credit card, my phone number, the numbers from *Lost*, the Fibonacci numbers, Pi to 100 places, Pamela Anderson's measurements, 58008 (which is boobs upside-down) and last week's Powerball, but none of them seemed to work. Finally, I tried my last resort: I yelled at the stereo while mashing all the buttons at the same time. Surprisingly, that didn't help either.

It was at this moment that the lovely man from roadside assistance (who I hadn't noticed was still there, and I suddenly felt very embarrassed about the shouting and mashing) suggested that I check the owner's manual for the code.

Brilliant idea! At last something was going right. Only one problem. Guess what? Turns out that when they robbed my car they also stole – drum roll please – the owner's manual. Well, either that or it had been eaten by the wet dog.

FOUR

SOMETHING OLD, SOMETHING NEW, SOMETHING BORROWED, SOMETHING BLUE

I don't want to seem mean-spirited, but it's always secretly pissed me off that when you go to a wedding, you're expected to take a present.

The fancy registry, in particular, gets my goat. Some couples seem to have confused getting married with winning the lot on *Sale of the Century*. Instead of 'I do', you expect them to say, 'I'll come back tomorrow night and play for the cars.'

Isn't it enough that they've found true love? Do they really need a toaster or a waffle iron thrown in to sweeten the deal?

'A stainless-steel potato-peeler. Now this truly is the most special day of my life.'

The truth is, I'm jealous. You see, while Amy and I have no plans to marry, it seems all our friends lately are taking the plunge – and the obligatory coffee plunger. Which begs the question: if we plan to stay together, but not get married, can we just have a day where we register at Myer and get all our married friends to deck out our house? And we don't plan to have kids either, so can we throw a baby shower for the cats?

Of course, the gifts don't stop on the wedding day – then come the wedding anniversaries. A couple of my mates celebrated their tenth recently, so I jumped online to find out what might be an appropriate gift. That's when I made a startling discovery.

Did you know they've updated the traditional wedding anniversary gifts? It's true. Let's start with the ten-year anniversary. In the good old days, if you made it to ten years, the appropriate gift was tin. But these days, some baked beans or Alphaghetti don't cut it. Tin has been replaced by – wait for it – diamonds.

It says something about the state of modern marriage that in the old days you had to wait sixty years for diamonds, but now, if you're lucky enough to make it to ten, it's time to crack out the bling. In fact, if you make it to ten years, you'd better ensure you're earning some good coin, because the next few years are going to cost you.

There are diamonds (ten), a girl's best friend; then fashion jewellery (eleven), a girl's best friend's best friend; then pearls (twelve), furs (thirteen) and gold jewellery (fourteen) – which, if they're not her best friends, they'd certainly be on her MySpace Top 10.

And it's not just the big anniversaries that are more costly. They've all changed. Traditionally, the first wedding anniversary was paper, so a card and a copy of a Sunday magazine had you covered. Actually, if you think about it, you didn't even need a present – just what you would have wrapped it in.

These days it's a bit more difficult. I suspect that if you tried to give your missus something made out of paper, the only papers you'd be getting in return would have the word 'divorce' on them. Apparently, nowadays the appropriate gift for the first anniversary is a clock. A clock isn't such a bad pressie – unless it's an egg-timer to measure your performance in the bedroom.

If you manage to make it to a second year, traditionally the gift was cotton, which meant you could basically cover it with a singlet. These days you're expected to fork out for china, which I think means plates and cups, not sweet and sour pork from the local takeaway.

The third-year anniversary used to be celebrated with leather, which makes me think that in the old days, if you managed to stick at your marriage for three years, things started to get a little kinky. Sadly, now you wait nine long years before the leather anniversary – perhaps it's an incentive to make marriages last longer. If this is the aim, they should change the tenth anniversary to 'jelly wrestling' and the twentieth to 'strippers'.

Today, the fourth anniversary is celebrated with appliances – fitting, because it's about the time when the warranties on all your wedding gifts expire and everything stops working. Traditionally this anniversary was celebrated with flowers. These days they're only the usual gift for blokes who forget their wedding anniversary.

All jokes aside, some of the changes are just plain silly. In the old days, the seventh anniversary was simple: wool. Nice. That could be anything from a fluffy jumper to a tea cosy. But do you know what they've replaced it with? No joke. Desk sets.

Desk sets? Can you believe it? How romantic. I know I've personally lost track of the number of Hallmark cards I've seen with, 'Roses are red, violets are blue, I've got a stapler, paperclip and Post-it note for you.' And are you looking for the perfect date movie for your anniversary? Then don't miss Hugh Grant's romantic comedy, *Four Weddings and a Desk Set*.

It's lucky I don't plan to get married, because I don't know how I'd afford the endless list of gifts. To be honest, I'm not great with money. My idea of investing is keeping all the loose change down the back of my couch for a rainy day. When it comes to belt-tightening, I've have always been the sort of guy who thought, 'Why tighten my belt when I can just buy a brand-new pair of pants that fit properly?'

I would have been hopeless on *The Price is Right*. When

SOMETHING OLD, SOMETHING NEW...

Larry asked me how much something cost I would have said, 'Ah, who cares? Just put it on my Amex and I'll worry about it later!'

My mate Dave (not his real name, for reasons that will become very obvious) is the opposite. He is – how can I put this nicely? – *frugal*. Like Kevin Rudd, Dave (NHRNFRTWBVO) would consider himself to be an 'economic conservative'. Most people would use another term, derived from the Latin *maximus tightius arseus*.

Yes, Dave is – like Thorpey's swimsuit would be if he tried to squeeze into it again these days – tight. And he's proud of it. When someone once told him he was so tight he'd only breathe in if he could, Dave got it printed on a T-shirt.

You know the old joke about someone opening their wallet and moths flying out? Well, that sums up Dave; except if he had moths living in his wallet he'd charge them rent. He's the sort of guy you don't take to the pub, because the only time he shouts is if there's a fire. (Although he has also been known to shout 'Fire!' if someone asks him for an expensive cocktail.)

But it's not just the pub. Oh no.

Take a drive with Dave and you'll learn that when he fills the car with petrol he always makes sure he shakes the hose until he gets to $20.02, because he knows they'll round down and he'll drive away with two cents worth of free fuel.

He also turns off his engine and whacks the car into neutral when he's at the top of steep hills because he thinks it saves him petrol. (To be honest, I'm surprised he hasn't cut the floor out of his car so he can power it like they do on *The Flintstones*.)

That's not all. Dave is the guy who once drove his car from Melbourne to Adelaide – not because it was cheaper than a plane, but because he had a boot filled with cans and bottles for the ten-cent deposit. And if you think that's bad, this is a guy who still went to O-Week five years after he graduated, just for the free condoms. (Although I have to be honest, I am kind of glad about that one, because he strikes me as the sort of guy who might have put used ones in the washing machine.)

Nothing comes as a surprise with Dave; after all, he's the guy who once pretended for two hours that he wanted to buy a flat-screen TV, just so he could watch the latest *Indiana Jones* film on the tellies at Harvey Norman.

Now, before you get the wrong idea, Dave is not a bad bloke. He just lives by the philosophy, 'Why pay for something when you can get it for free?' When we were at uni he survived an entire month on a 'toothpick diet' – eating only the free samples handed out in supermarkets and food courts. He said it was like constantly being at a cocktail party.

And the entire time I've known him he's never owned aftershave, but always smells great. When I asked him what he was wearing one day, he said, 'Free tester.'

But the best example was when he agreed to pick me up at the airport to save me getting a cab (generous gesture), but then paged me over the loudspeaker to avoid having to call me on his mobile.

SOMETHING OLD, SOMETHING NEW...

The other night Dave invited me to a barbie at his house. Now it goes without saying that all barbecues at Dave's are BYOB (Bring Your Own Booze) and BYOMOSS (Bring Your Own Meat or Soy Substitute). I won't be surprised if one day it is also BYOBBQ. It was only when I asked for some good old-fashioned tomato sauce to go with my soy-sage that I realised how absolutely tight-tanic Dave had become.

'No worries,' he said, reached into his pocket and produced a range of packages marked Tomato Sauce, Mustard and Mayo. 'I stole them from Hungry Jack's,' he said proudly. 'Oh wait, there's more.' He shoved his hand in further and pulled out some sugar, sweetener, salt and pepper.

That's when I realised that a) the reason some restaurants don't let you touch the pepper-grinder is because of people like Dave, and b) if I ever get caught with a suspicious package of white powder in my pocket, I want it to be something cooler than Splenda.

These days Dave buys in bulk. The first time I saw his pantry I thought it was a nuclear bomb shelter (although with the amount of baked beans he had, I think the most dangerous explosions would have been coming from the inside). But given the dire state of our economy, perhaps Dave is just being sensible and responsible. Maybe in these harsh economic times the fact that I don't like to re-use my teabags is the equivalent of lighting cigars with hundred-dollar notes.

One thing's for sure: Dave is probably the only person I know who would manage to survive on the pension.

Seriously, if the true measure of a society is the way we treat our elderly, I think our report card should read 'Must try harder'. Did you know that the average pensioner has to make do with a grand total of $264 a week, give or take a few piddly allowances? It's an amount I'm ashamed to say I wouldn't think twice about splurging on a new pair of jeans or sunglasses. (Which I guess explains why you see so few nannas swanning about in Sass & Bide pants and Dolce sunnies.)

Now, to some people $264 might seem like a decent amount, but once you take out the essentials like housing, amenities and medical expenses, you're left with bugger-all before you can even think about food and bingo.

Which got me thinking: which items that I take for granted would I have to renounce if I were living on the pension? I decided to try it for a fortnight and find out.

Now, let me say that I realise living on the pension for only two weeks is kind of like playing a weekend of paintball and expecting to march on Anzac Day. But those two weeks at least gave me a small insight into the battles our pensioners face every day.

The first thing I learned is why pensioners are so excited about a lunchtime gig by Kamahl at the local RSL – it's free. When you're on a pension budget, entertainment expenses are the first item to go out the window. Gone was my Foxtel and internet, and going to the movies or even hiring a DVD was a pipe dream. By the end of the two weeks I was loitering

SOMETHING OLD, SOMETHING NEW...

in the local Harvey Norman just to get my DVD fix on the big screen.

The next thing I discovered is how difficult it is to get about. Gone was my car – I couldn't afford the upkeep or rego – and if I'd filled the tank the vehicle would have doubled in value.

Then there was the big one: food. Gone were the daily coffees and buying my lunch at work. (I was starting to realise why some pensioners can seem a little grumpy; it's the hunger pains and caffeine withdrawals. By the end of week one I was telling teenagers to pull up their pants and was convinced there wasn't a problem in the world that couldn't be solved by a good dose of national service.)

And while I could certainly find things in my budget in the supermarket, I ate more two-minute noodles and baked beans in that fortnight than I had in the last two years. In fact, if I'd eaten any more beans I would have saved money on amenities by producing my own natural gas.

By the end of the two weeks, my food budget was so tight I had to steal milk from the fridge at work, I was skipping meals (was I living like a pensioner or a supermodel?) and attending functions for the free finger food. At one party, the girl with the canapés thought I was stalking her. I was contemplating lining my pockets with Glad Bags so I could take some food home.

Speaking of doggy bags, I don't know where this myth about pensioners eating pet-food comes from: it's much more expensive than regular food. If I were forced to spend another two weeks on the pension, the cats would have either had to learn to enjoy the taste of two-minute noodles, or I would have had to eat them.

So was I able to last two weeks on $264 a week? Well, despite my budgeting and stealing, I still ran out of money before the end of the fortnight, and I certainly learned just how many little things I take for granted. From now on I'll certainly put a little extra money in my super fund each week – or maybe I should start smoking to reduce my lifespan? And next time it's my nanna's birthday, I'm going to put $5 in the card instead of the other way around.

It also reminded me how lucky I am to have a job – largely because I got it under so many false pretences that it's a wonder they trust me with anything at all. I spent the first few weeks in the office scared stiff that all the lies in my résumé would be uncovered.

Like when I said I had an 'excellent history of computer skills', what I really meant was I used to be a gun at playing Pong on my Commodore 64. And when I suggested I possessed 'great communication skills', I meant I planned to spend most of my time at work using the company phone for personal calls and googling my own name. (And I probably should mention that when I said I was a 'team player', it meant I'd spend most Monday mornings reading the paper to see how my team played.)

Oh, and don't even get me started on my claim that I can

SOMETHING OLD, SOMETHING NEW...

speak 'several languages'. If they find out these languages are Australian and Pig Latin then I am otallytay ootedray.

Although I do stand by my suggestion that I 'get on well with others' – but this simply means I'm likely to get drunk at the office Christmas party and try to pash someone in the stationery cupboard. Hey, there's nothing sexier than a strategically placed Post-it note.

But getting on well with others is definitely one of the most important skills in any new gig, so in the first few weeks I tried my best to make a good impression by smiling at everyone who walked past my desk.

Unfortunately, it seemed I might have been trying a little too hard, because half the office assumed I was on drugs, and the other half was concerned I was deranged and just looking for an opportunity to throw them into a hole in my basement and make them 'rub the lotion on their skin'.

One of the toughest things for me, as you'd expect, was remembering everybody's name. There were days when I wished I worked at McDonald's, because at least everyone wears name tags there. (And it's easy to remember that the boss's name is Ronald.)

For the first few weeks I simply referred to pretty much everyone I saw as 'mate' – which was fine until a bunch of them walked by together and I found myself nodding my head and saying, 'Mate...mate...mate...mate.' You could've easily assumed that either I had a really bad stutter or I was doing an impression of a seagull searching for chips.

To make matters worse, because I didn't know who was who, I ended up doing stupid things like asking the CEO to get me a cup of coffee, and then spending two hours bonding with a courier who'd popped into the building to drop off a package. And can someone please tell me why the first person I make friends with in any office is the woman who has seventy-two cats and a mug that says, 'You don't have to be mad to work here ... but it helps'?

But I think the single hardest thing for me about any new job is finding my way around the office. I have such a bad sense of direction that in my first week I barely left my desk – I was terrified that if I went to the toilet I wouldn't be able to find my way back again. (And apparently they think it's weird if you leave a breadcrumb trail.)

Speaking of loos, you know you've scored the bad office when it's not only next to the toilet, but you start to suspect it may well have *been* the toilet. Especially when your chair comes with a half-flush and full-flush option; the fax paper holder is a toilet-paper dispenser; and on the blackboard is written, 'For a good time call ...'

However, as we all know, the vital thing about getting your bearings at a new job is finding out where all the important things are kept ... so you can start stealing them. I know I shouldn't endorse it, but I love a bit of workplace pilfering. It's always fascinated me that people who would never ever steal anything in the real world suddenly turn into Winona Ryder the minute they walk through the office doors. (I haven't read the Bible closely, but apparently the commandment is actually, 'Thou Shalt Not Steal – Except at Work, Those Bastards Deserve It.')

One of my mates (yes, you guessed who) has pretty much furnished his house with stuff he nicked from his office. Even when he makes you a simple cup of tea, you know he's using stolen tea served in a stolen mug using water boiled from a stolen kettle and stirred with a stolen teaspoon. (The real giveaway is when you ask for sugar and he gives you sachets.)

My soft spot is stationery. When I walk into the stationery cupboard I'm like Augustus Gloop in Willy Wonka's chocolate factory. That said, I do have some standards. I figure it's OK to steal a couple of notebooks, but nicking a couple of notebook computers is crossing a line. That said, when I lost my last job I did contemplate stealing a photocopier piece by piece. I imagined myself shaking parts out of the bottom of my pants each day, as though I was in *The Great Escape.*

I got through my anxiety-ridden first weeks by telling myself that if the new gig didn't work out, I could always start my own Officeworks – because seriously, I have no idea what I'm going to do with all that stationery piled up in my lounge room . . .

While we're on the subject of things we *think* we need but really don't . . . well, I have a confession to make: I drive a 4WD.

Yes, dear readers, I am indeed one of those road-hogging,

petrol-guzzling, environment-destroying, talk-on-the-mobile-while-driving, complete and utter tossers who drives a 4WD in the city.

Hi, my name is Wil, and I am a tool. For some reason even I can't seem to remember why, when I went to buy my car, I decided I needed an off-road vehicle. This is despite the fact that in the seven years since I purchased my 4WD, the only time I've even come close to venturing off-road is when I completely buggered up a reverse park and ended up on the nature strip.

The only bush-bashing I ever do involves the former American president, and the closest I've ever come to driving through creeks or bursting through sand-dunes is when I occasionally forget to slow down for a speed bump.

I feel increasingly stupid driving a 4WD, given I never take it into the country. I mean, I wouldn't wear an Akubra, R.M. Williams and a Driza-bone into the office.

Did you know that these days you can buy spray-on dirt to give your 4WD that off-road look even if you've never taken it off-road? (It's also a good substitute if you can't afford spray-on tan.)

I mean, I live in the city: why do I need the power of a 4WD? So I can get to the next set of traffic lights faster than the people around me? Most mornings during peak hour I never even manage to get my speedo above fifty. I don't need a 4WD — I barely need a fourth gear. I don't need a V6, I could probably run my car on a couple of cans of V.

SOMETHING OLD, SOMETHING NEW ...

I'm not a blokey bloke, I don't care how many killer-wasps my car has. I just care if it has cup-holders.

Sure, there's the possibility that at some stage I might venture off-road, but using that logic, I should drive a tank on the off-chance that at some stage I might have to go to war. Me having a 4WD is kind of like me remaining single on the off-chance I might at some stage get to meet Scarlett Johansson.

So why did I buy one? Well, I guess like a lot of people, I got sucked in by the promise of the lifestyle it might offer me. All the cars have such adventurous names, like the Territory and the Land Cruiser and the Outlander and the Penis Extension. I reckon people would be less likely to be sucked into buying one if they were named after what you *really* end up doing in them. Like the Ford Pick-the-Kids-Up-from-School, the Toyota Change-Lanes-Without-Indicating and the Mitsubishi Can't-Reverse-Park.

It's the promise of off-road adventure that sucks you in when you buy a 4WD. It's that idea of being half-city, half-country. Someone once described the mullet haircut as business up the top and party down the back, and that's what people think when they buy one of these planet-polluting monsters. (Actually, now that I think about it, that wouldn't be a bad name for a car: the Mazda Mullet.)

That's why all the ads feature the standard creek shots, desert donuts and parking perilously close to the edge of a cliff. The nearest most 4WD drivers will ever come to a cliff is if that's the name of the pensioner they knock down at the crossing while talking on their mobile phone.

And with petrol prices rising so fast, it's soon going to be cheaper to put champagne in your tank and save the unleaded to drink on special occasions. It's becoming more and more ridiculous to drive my gas-guzzling beast. If thieves broke into my four-wheeler, the most valuable thing they could steal would be my fuel. If petrol prices go up any more, I might finally get to take my car off-road – I'll have to invade Iraq myself to get some cheap oil.

At this point, you might be asking why, if I really hate 4WDs so much, I don't just trade mine in for something more fuel-efficient and practical? Well, I think about it, but then I come back to one thing – safety. My safety.

You see, I am a terrible, terrible driver, and deep down I have the selfish mindset that if I have an accident in my 4WD, at least the other person will come off worse than I will. I'm hopeless. I have so many accidents that my friends printed me some bumper stickers that say, 'I got rear-ended by Wil Anderson and all I got was this lousy sticker!'

Those companies that have started advertising on car airbags must have me as their target audience. (Yes, that's right, airbags. Apparently it's the latest marketing trend.) I guess I should tell them that they're wasting their time. Despite my weakness for a bit of retail therapy, even I don't think of shopping the minute I have an accident: 'Hmmm, I know I've just been in a serious life-threatening prang, but for some

SOMETHING OLD, SOMETHING NEW . . .

reason I'm craving a Big Mac. Oh, I know what it is. It must be those giant golden arches that are now embedded . . . in . . . my . . . forehead.'

Seriously, what sort of companies want their products advertised on airbags? Insurance? Headache tablets? Tow-trucks? New cars? Or maybe just a better prescription for your glasses?

Still, if I've learned one thing about the world of advertising, it's that the more far-fetched something seems, the greater the likelihood that someone is thinking about doing it. Honestly, if they could, most ad gurus would happily tattoo logos to the insides of our eyelids, so that every time we blinked we'd get a subliminal message.

So, assuming the airbag ads are legit, what next? Will we see ads on the lids of coffins, so even the deceased can be targeted? 'Dead tired? Why not try a Red Bull?'

I know that for some people ads are the gaps in the show that allow them to put on the kettle or duck to the bathroom, but I've always been fascinated by the power of the persuaders. After all, if they can convince us to buy the purple washing liquid over the green, what else can they do?

One of the main motivators they use to sell us CWPDN (crap we probably don't need) is fear. And before you start saying, 'Well, we live in a free market Wil, and if you don't like it why don't you and all your latte-sipping ABC mates get on a boat to Russia', all I'm asking is, do we really need to make people feel bad in order to sell them stuff?

There are ads for health insurance, car insurance, house insurance, dog-house insurance and insurance against getting a paper-cut while filling out your insurance. Turn on the telly for about half an hour and before long you'll be convinced that someone is going to steal your house, burn down your car and go for a joy-ride in your dog. No wonder we watch so many crime shows. We just want to see someone murdered to know they're worse off than we are.

But the ads that really make my blood boil are the ones – usually for cleaning products – that drum home the message, 'Buy this or you are a bad parent.'

Now, I'm the first to acknowledge that there are plenty of ways to be a bad parent, but buying the wrong brand of toilet duck doesn't rank high on my list.

I can't imagine someone saying, 'My old man was a real bastard. He drank too much, had affairs and clipped us around the ears regularly . . . but at least he bought the lemon-scented Spray & Wipe.'

There's one particular fear-based ad that gives me a case of the very thing it's used to clean up. I think you'll know the ad. It's the one where a woman has some friends and family coming to visit and suddenly realises she hasn't cleaned the toilet.

The clear implication seems to be that if she doesn't quickly use the particular cleaning product in question, her friends will see her dirty bathroom, judge her, reject her friendship and quite possibly march her through the main street of town to the chant of 'Unclean . . . unclean!'

SOMETHING OLD, SOMETHING NEW...

Now, while everyone likes a clean bathroom, isn't this just a tad extreme? I mean, if my mates are going to dump me because my toilet isn't clean enough to eat off, then good. Yes, that's right, good. Better I find out how fairweather they are now, before they uncover the really disturbing stuff about me.

While we're being honest, I have to confess I've never understood the supposed compliment, 'She has a toilet so clean you could eat off it!' I don't care how clean the toilet is, if someone wants me to have dinner on their dunny, then thank you very much but I'll eat at home. I would much rather someone had a dirty toilet but allowed me to eat off the table.

Yes, there's no doubt that certain people get a little too enthusiastic about cleaning up. But overzealous homebodies are one thing; recently I was the victim of a clean-up that had far more malevolent overtones.

A few weeks ago, thieves broke into my car and stole a bag that had my wallet in it. In doing so, they managed to take off with my driver's licence, three credit cards (my main one, and the other two I use to pay off my main one), my ATM card, my Medicare card and my Frequent Flyer and NRMA cards. They also took my Western Bulldogs Football Club membership card, but it was finals time, so that one no longer had any value.

They cleaned out my ashtrays, too. Of loose change, that is. Imagine if thieves broke into your car and all they took were the ciggie butts and empty Coke cans? It would be like being carjacked by Ian Kiernan.

At first I thought I was pretty lucky; after all, the only other things of real value they took were my two iPods. So they're out of luck if they're massive Shannon Noll fans. But what I assumed was a straightforward robbery started to seem a little more intriguing when I took a closer look.

They'd taken the complete third series of *House* on DVD – although I say more fool them, as it's going to have absolutely no value unless they nicked the first two from someone else. However, they left behind my Danny Bhoy stand-up DVD. Danny shouldn't feel too rejected. They're not worth having as fans, because even if they really liked his comedy they'd probably mug an unsuspecting punter for a ticket rather than pay for one.

Also gone was my Holden stubby-holder (obviously we can rule out Ford fans) and, more intriguingly, a pair of Australian-flag socks I had bought at the airport and never worn. So I guess we can assume that the thieves were either extremely patriotic, or had cold feet and some even colder beers.

That's not all. They had also emptied the glove box of my sunglasses and a pair of fingerless gloves (does that make it a fingerless-glove box?). And last but not least, they'd nicked the bottle of aftershave I keep in there for putting on after a jog. So if I ever need to identify the robbers in a line-up, I might be able to sniff them out: 'Yes, it's definitely number three ... the guy with the distinct odour of Vera Wang For Men.'

So, on first assessment, not too bad. In the grand scheme of things, I reckoned I'd lost nothing that couldn't be replaced. But then a new thought came crashing in: I realised that the bag also contained my passport — and I was meant to be leaving the country in less than three days.

In a panic I immediately rang the passport office, who told me that they could issue me an emergency replacement as long as I could bring some form of ID, such as my driver's licence, credit cards or Medicare card. Oh crap ...

I grabbed a bunch of bills from home, jumped into my now quite roomy car, and headed for the RTA. I figured if I could just get my driver's licence, I could then go to the bank and sort out money, and then I could replace my passport. Simple.

Or so I thought. I'd barely pulled my car into the street when the orange petrol light started flashing, telling me I was about to run out of petrol. Now, normally there's a simple solution to this — put petrol in the car. But as you might have guessed, I didn't have any money, not even the loose change I usually keep in the ashtray. (And I was pretty sure the petrol station wouldn't take a Danny Bhoy DVD as barter, since even the thieves rejected it.)

Luckily, my trip was mostly downhill and I pulled up out the front of the RTA and rushed inside hoping it wouldn't take long, especially as I couldn't get a parking ticket because I had no coins.

As it turned out, parking tickets were my major undoing. When it was my turn to be served they told me they couldn't renew my licence until I settled an unpaid fine. On the upside, it was only forty bucks, but on the downside I didn't have forty bucks, and I couldn't put it on my credit card because I couldn't get one without ID.

I had no choice but to go to the bank and try my luck. To their credit, they were very keen to help. In fact, there was only one snag – they just needed to see one piece of photo ID: a passport, a driver's license, a library card, anything. Anything.

And then it struck me. I rushed out to my car, reached under the seat and groped around in hope. There it was: my book *Survival of the Dumbest*, which had my name and a huge photo of me on the front.

I ran back into the bank and pleaded, 'Will this do?' The guy looked at me and said, 'It wouldn't normally, but I guess it's probably easier to obtain a fake ID than to go to the effort of writing a book and getting it published, so I'm going to trust you.'

Once I had some money, the rest was simple. I paid off my fine, got my licence, ordered new credit cards and even managed to get my passport one full day before my plane was due to leave the country. With that out of the way, I could focus on replacing my Australian socks and Holden stubby-holder at duty-free.

For some blokes, duty-free shopping is about the only kind they like – all that cheap booze and those giant packs of cigarettes and chocolates. But unlike most Aussie men, I actually quite like shopping – yes, even with my girlfriend. I particularly like buying her new clothes; although if a dress is really expensive, I do warn her that I'll have to wear it on stage at least once so I can claim it on my tax.

I know that as a general rule, blokes aren't that excited about seeing women try on clothes; we're more interested in seeing them take them off. If it were the other way around, on their bucks' nights, bachelors wouldn't end up at a strip-club, they'd end up at a get-dressed club. 'Oh yeah, baby, put on a jumper, yeah, and a jacket too. Now, if I tuck $5 into your thermal undies, will you put on a scarf and beanie for me? Oh yeah, you're hot now!'

Women, on the other hand, love to take their partners shopping because it combines two of their favourite activities – buying stuff and seeing their partner miserable.

I'm just kidding; as I've said, I quite like shopping. It's just that men and women shop so differently. Women will happily window-shop for hours, whereas the only time you'll hear a man say he's going window-shopping is when he has a big hole in the wall of his house and he needs a sheet of glass to stop the breeze blowing over his beer.

Men shop like they've just won *Wheel of Fortune*: 'I'll have one of those . . . one of those . . . one of those . . . and one of those!' 'But sir, that last one was our shop assistant Tiffany!' 'Good, she can help carry the other stuff home. Does she come in blonde?'

Most fancy shops these days cater for the dragged-along dude, and have a 'man area' with a couch or stool set aside. There's nothing worse than having to linger out the front. Sometimes I get so bored, to amuse myself I start spruiking: 'We have ladies' shoes $2, we have dresses $2, everything must go!' Of course, the women get pissed off when they walk into the shop and discover that nothing costs less than $200.

But I think they could take the man comfort thing a little further. If they installed an Xbox and a bar fridge, women could shop for as long as they wanted. 'No seriously, honey, try on something else. I just want to finish this level.' At the very least, they could invest in some bloke-centric magazines. Have you seen those *Harry Potter* books with different covers for adults? They should do that with magazines, so the outside looks like *Vogue* or *Marie Claire* but inside they're *FHM* and the form guide.

What's most embarrassing is when your partner is in the change room and she asks you to get the dress in another size. When I ask the shop assistant, 'Do you have this in a 2?' I always imagine they're staring at me thinking, 'First of all, you're a bloke, and second, there's no way you're a size 2.'

But shopping for clothes isn't all Dinnigan shenanigans and Issey Miyake malarky. A lot of the time it can be really disheartening, mostly because the clothes never seem to look as good on as they do on the models. (Although I do have bigger boobs than Kate Moss.) I've always thought designers would be better off putting clothes on the ugliest, most out-of-shape models they can find. That way when you try stuff on, at least you'd look good by comparison. 'Wow, these jeans make my bum look big, but nowhere near as big as that lard-arse.'

Another thing that confuses me about women's clothes is the sizes. From shop to shop the same person can be a 12, a 34 and a 2. It's less like they're sizing dresses and more like they're reading out the numbers on Lotto. (On the upside, it does make you feel good when in one shop you're a 12 and in the next you're a 1. 'Wow, 11 sizes in 10 steps . . . Stick that in your Speedos, Jenny Craig!')

Then, of course, there's the holy grail of women's shopping: shoes. I know it's a cliché, but women lust over shoes as though they're made of gold and polished with George Clooney's sweat. I've now decided that the female shoe fetish represents a wonderful opportunity for men. Blokes spend much of their time trying to attract women, but I say forget the car you drive, the job you have or even the aftershave you wear. If you really want to get a woman into your pants, it's simple – just shove a pair of Manolo Blahniks down the front of your daks.

Personally, I can't see the appeal of walking around in a pair of shoes that makes a night of bondage seem like an Ayurvedic massage. As for my own fashion style, I'd describe it as 'comfortable'. Others have more unkindly labelled it 'homeless chic'. The sad thing is, they're probably a little closer to the truth.

I have to be honest, sometimes when I venture out of the house the only thing separating me from the permanently-dwelling-challenged is a cardboard sign that reads, 'Will tell jokes for food!' Forget watches and man-bags, the only thing that would complement my clothes is some cymbals between my knees and a couple of ice-cream containers for drums. Pretty much every photo I have of myself looks like it's been ripped from a *New Weekly* Stars Without Their Make-up (and Dignity) special.

Fashion experts say the way you present yourself says something about you, even before you speak. I think most of my outfits say either, 'Keep me away from children' or 'Would you like to buy *The Big Issue*?'

When some people choose clothes, they dress to feel sexy, fashionable or stylish. I like to dress to feel ... comfy. Put it this way, I have never met a pair of tracksuit pants I didn't like. Forget the debate about whether the high waist or the low waist is in this season; I only care about the elastic waist. I don't care about 'the new black', I care about 'the new track(ies)'.

My problem with John Howard was never that he wore the Wallabies tracksuit when he went on his early-morning power-walks. It was that he didn't wear it all the time. When the world leaders came to Australia for APEC, forget the Akubras and Driza-bones: I would have liked to see them decked out in the green and gold trackies. I bet everyone in the room would have been a lot happier and in the mood to negotiate if, after a long official lunch, they didn't have to let their belts out a couple of notches.

That's the thing about tracksuit pants: they're forgiving. If you buy a pair of skinny jeans and put on a couple of kilos, your legs end up looking like someone's trying to squeeze icing onto a cake. Tracksuit pants don't even notice if you've gained weight; they're the best friend you'll never have. Whether you need them for a jog or yoga, nursing a hangover or getting over a broken relationship sitting on the couch eating icing sugar and crying at Sorbent ads, they'll be there to support and comfort you.

And tracksuit pants don't demand much in return. They don't need to be dry-cleaned or steam-cleaned or hung or folded like some 'needy' clothes. Just pick them up from the floor where you left them the night before, give them a quick sniff test, and away you go.

I think I love trackies so much, I would even consider getting married wearing them. Of course, the only downside to that master plan is that if you're the sort of person who thinks it's OK to wear tracksuit pants to a wedding, chances are nobody is ever going to marry you.

Yes, suits may look good, but they are bloody uncomfortable. Nobody has ever said, 'I'll join you to veg out on the couch in a minute, but I just want to change into my three-piece Armani.' Personally, my idea of getting dressed up is putting on my good tracksuit pants (the ones that have the rope-tie at the waist as well as the elastic) and making sure they don't have any suspicious stains on them.

Sometimes I secretly suspect I chose my job not because I like telling jokes, but because I hate wearing pants. Every day is casual clothes Friday at my place. I have only two suits in my entire wardrobe, and they're reserved for what I call 'the big Cs': corporate gigs and court appearances.

But even as a stand-up comedian, I have to confess that it's hard to get away with wearing tracksuits at shows or on the telly without people starting to think you've completely given up on life.

In fact, unless you work at home, I think there are only two jobs where it's OK to wear trackies all the time – professional sportsperson and professional drug dealer. Clearly, tracksuit pants need a PR campaign and a slogan. And so I thought I would come up with one:

> They are comfy and dependable, and I think they're cute,
> This is my ode to the humble tracksuit.
> They are warm and yet stylish, there is nothing sinister,
> Worn by humble workers, sports stars and even prime ministers.
> And if you are worried that they make you look crapper,
> Then just add some bling and they become gangsta rapper.
> You can wear them all day, and there will be no dramas,
> And then wear them to bed and they become pyjamas.
> You can wear them while sober, drunk, awake or asleep,

SOMETHING OLD, SOMETHING NEW . . .

Oh, and did I forget to mention they are bloody cheap?
They really are super, the humble tracksuits,
If combined with some thongs or even ugg boots.
So whether you're Carl Williams or on *So You Think You Can Dance?*
Let's all stand and salute the wonder that is trackie pants.

❊ ❊ ❊

I don't mind accompanying my girlfriend to the local mall or shopping strip, but I do draw the line at market-shopping.

Don't get me wrong, I don't mind the occasional wander around, but when I contemplate ways to spend a lazy Sunday, I'm less likely to be the little piggy who went to market and more likely to be the little piggy who stayed home nursing a hangover on the couch, happily reading newspapers and watching sport.

Because let's face it folks, when your mum played 'This little piggy' with you as a kid, she never mentioned that the little piggy would end up spending most of the day bartering with hippies and coming home with a whole load of useless crap like driftwood picture frames and garden gnomes made out of old coathangers.

But I digress.

In my experience, your average market shopping trip can be broken into three categories: arts and crafts, clothes and food.

First cab off the rank, arts and crafts markets tend to consist of handicraft stalls, woodcraft stalls, incense and perfume stalls, and of course the stuff-we-found-lying-around-our-house-but-couldn't-be-buggered-taking-to-Cash-Converters stall.

For some reason these markets always seem to be populated predominantly by people who make their own candles – probably because with the money they earn at the markets they can't afford electricity. There are stalls filled with coloured candles, scented candles and candles that remove all the wax from your ears – to which they add a wick and make more candles.

The candle cavalcade is rivalled only by the hippies flogging homemade soap. These guys look like they should spend a little more time using the stuff themselves and a little less trying to sell it to unsuspecting strangers. The soaps always seem to contain 'essential oils', which makes me wonder: if they are indeed so essential, how come I have survived thirty-five years without them?

But at least these products have some practical application, as opposed to the myriad stalls run by people whose ultimate dream is to be the next Tonia Todman. I'm referring to the collection of ashtrays, wind chimes, doorstops and assorted knick-knacks created by people who clearly got their inspiration from watching egg cartons, toilet rolls and pipe cleaners assembled to make things on *Play School*, thinking, 'Wow, this could be my next career!'

SOMETHING OLD, SOMETHING NEW...

Next up we have the clothes markets. While you can often find some awesome stuff, most of the time it's like trying to find a needle in a haystack, or a funny joke in a Rob Schneider film.

For starters, there are the handmade clothes – mostly hand-woven hippie pants and tie-dyed T-shirts that you could only really wear if you were running a stall at the markets ... or joining the lucrative professional fire-twirling circuit.

Then there are the second-hand, or third-hand, or fourth-, fifth- and sixth-hand clothes that often smell like the last owner stopped wearing them when they were removed at the morgue. These are usually sold in stalls with no mirrors at all, which seems deliberate to me: they don't want you to realise how bad you look until you get home; either that, or their main clientele are vampires.

And while we're on the topic, when did the word 'vintage' replace the word 'old'? These days there's no such thing as an old or second-hand piece of clothing at the market, it's all vintage. If you want to know the difference: when something is 'old' it means you can buy it for half its original price, but if something is 'vintage' you usually get charged double. It's pretty clever marketing if you think about it. I mean, no-one would ever buy old wine, but call it vintage and suddenly it's a collector's item.

Maybe others could take this advice on board. Old King Cole could reinvent himself as Vintage King Cole; the Bible could relaunch the Vintage Testament; and I'm sure your parents wouldn't be as annoyed if you shipped them off to a Vintage Folks' Home.

Last but not least is my favourite kind of market: the food markets. I don't know what it is, but in my opinion food always tastes better when it's prepared by a sweaty guy in the back of a caravan using implements most illegal speed labs would consider too unhygienic. Plus, I have to confess there's nothing like scouring the fresh food markets for perfect organic produce that you can then take home and watch rot in your fruit bowl for the next two weeks.

However, the local market is no place for anyone with a nut allergy, as there are guaranteed to be more hot nuts than there are in the loincloths at a Sumo tournament.

But the great thing about a food market is, it's one of the few places left in the world where you can buy juice off a grumpy person – as opposed to the franchises where the kids are so happy, you suspect the secret ingredient they boost their juice with is ecstasy.

There are, of course, some things that you are guaranteed to see at all markets, regardless of category. At every market there will be someone painting kids' faces, which means that by the end of the day the market will resemble a midget version of *Braveheart*.

At every market there will be some old hippie in the corner selling *How to Grow Your Own Pot* books, homemade smoking paraphernalia, and assorted knitting patterns for bong cosies. Every market will have at least one kid playing a musical instrument extremely badly and hitting notes that only local dogs can hear. This, in turn, means that every market will also have a group of confused punters torn between tossing some money in the tiny busker's hat and not wanting to reward mediocrity.

And finally, at every market you'll ever attend you'll find an incense stall, which is perfect for covering the smell of most of the people selling stuff – and a great place to stand after visiting the curry hut, Hey Hey, It's Satay Day! Don't you just love that name? Honestly, it was enough to make a day at the markets worthwhile.

In fact, I think it's time we paid tribute to those small business owners who aren't satisfied to simply start a business, but also aim to bring some much-needed joy to the world by giving it a pun name.

If your car breaks down, who are you going to call? Boring old roadside assistance? Or will you pick up your phone and call CamelTow or Lord of the Dings? If you need a bed in Blackburn, are you going to pop down to Capt'n Snooze, where even the name puts you to sleep, or to a place called 'Back to the Futon' – and then grab the bedding at Holy Sheet?

If you want to help the environment by installing a water tank, why not save the planet with a smile by popping into Tanks a Lot, or Tanks for the Memories?

I hope you never have the misfortune of getting stuck in an elevator, but if you do, who are you going to buzz? The police? The fire-brigade? I don't think so. Not when you can call Schindler's Lifts.

And if you'd like a new tattoo, why get some shaky biker to apply your ink when you can pop down to Braybrook and get yourself some Tattatude?

One of the best pun shop names I have ever seen was a souvenir place in Edinburgh called 'Thistle Do Nicely'. And sure, the women from *Sex and the City* might love buying shoes, but so should the people of South Australia when they pop into the wonderfully named R. Soles.

When it comes to pun names, it seems some industries are fonder of them than others. For example, hairdressers quite often go to a great deal of effort to dream up a punny name. I used to live right near a barber in Fitzroy called The Bald and the Beautiful. But I've also seen Do Yer Nut in Redcliffe, Barber Blacksheep, and every second town seems to have a Curl Up and Dye.

Asian restaurants are also famous for giving it a good crack, from Thairiffic to Thai Me Kangaroo Down Sport, plus Wok and Roll in Queensland, the Hard Wok Café in Sydney, and my personal favourite, Pho Shizzle in the USA.

But maybe Asian food isn't your thing, and you're more in the mood for some good old-fashioned fish and chips. Well then, it's time to head north to Queensland to visit The Codfather or A Salt and Battery. Then there's Seafood and Eat It in the Blue Mountains, Prawn Star at Avoca Beach, or why not just pop into Lord of the Fries. (Or if you want to catch

SOMETHING OLD, SOMETHING NEW...

the fish yourself, head to Benalla and visit the Master Baiter Tackle Shop.)

What if you're jonesing for a simple pizza. Who are you going to call? Pizza Hut? Dominos? Not when you can place an order at Pizza the Action!

Everyone in Melbourne should pop down to St Kilda for an a icy-cold beer at the Dick Whittington, but I'm not so sure you'll be salivating if you opt for the drive-through and see the sign, The Dick Liquor.

Want to buy some plants? Maybe it's time to get your butt to Toowong to visit the nursery Aloe Aloe. If you just need a romantic bunch of flowers, I'd recommend either Florist Gump, Petallica or Austin Flowers.

If you really love your wordplay and want to have some pun in the sun, I recommend a trip down the Great Ocean Road to Ocean Grove. There you will find the best-named grocer of all-time: Elvis Parsley and Grapesland. Now that's a name that would have encouraged The King himself to eat some fruit.

My fascination with words and wordplay also extends to newspaper headlines. In fact, often reading the article spoils the story for me. Sometimes, just for fun, I'll scan the headlines and form my wild (and probably completely inaccurate) opinions from there. After all, why let the facts get in the way of an interesting story?

On the good days it's like shooting fish in a barrel. The other day, for instance, the front page headline screamed: 'Mike Munro films prostate exam.' Well, I thought, that would have been a pretty easy exam, because I've never seen a bigger arsehole. It was official confirmation of what we've all believed for a long time – that he really is full of shit.

And they filmed it for TV, too. Doesn't that give a whole new meaning to 'hole in the wall'? Maybe if it's successful they'll turn it into a franchise: 'Prostate exams with the stars.'

Even serious headlines make me laugh. Like the one that trumpeted, 'WHO declares swine flu pandemic'. Wow, I thought, can't wait until *Who Weekly* declares its 25 Hottest Swine Flu Sufferers Without Their Make-Up.

Or yet another football scandal: 'NRL player charged $50,000 for having girl in his room'. Now that's an impressive first date. I thought I was doing well if I paid for dinner. But is this really going to stop the problems in the NRL? Surely next time he'll invite his mates to join him, so he can split the bill.

This headline sat neatly next to another of my favourites: 'NRL sponsor pulls out'. Good, I thought, now all we need is to convince players to not put it in in the first place.

And who can forget this one: 'Sam Newman calls for Matt Johns' reinstatement'. Good on him for supporting a mate, but isn't that kinda like trying to get council building approval with a reference from Josef Fritzl?

Another of my favourite pastimes is to complete the headline. For example: '*Twilight* star Robert Pattinson hit by taxi' – taxidriver then beaten to death by fourteen-year-old girls. Or 'Andre and Jordan split' — she gets half his abs, he gets one boob; or 'Bondi on the River Thames recreates real Bondi' — apparently it's impossible to get a park nearby and it's full of drunk English people. What about 'Live crabs stored in restaurant toilet' — man says, 'See, I told my doctor you could get crabs from the toilet'; or 'US network commissions reincarnation show' — will they call it *Thank Buddha You're Here ... Again*?; or 'Footy club to drop All White Night' — albinos reportedly devastated at the news; or 'Hell's Angels fear image isn't hardcore enough' — plan to either bring in shoot to kill or ban *Gossip Girl* night; or 'Mel Gibson divorce shock' — she blames irreconcilable differences, he blames the Jews. 'Octomum gets own TV show'? Personally, I'd like to see her present the lotto: she could pop out six balls and two supplementaries. '*All Saints* suffers budget cuts' — now it resembles an actual hospital; or even 'Gambler blew 2 million in 43 minutes' — Paris Hilton says, 'Wow ... his jaw must have really ached after that.'

Speaking of which, it's become a cliché to say that sex sells, but when it comes to putting the head back into headlines, it certainly delivers more than a mouthful. Consider these recent stories:

'Blaze at nude swingers resort'. Yes folks, it's a real story; apparently firefighters were called to put out several bushfires.

'Jamaican dance results in broken penises'. Can't wait to see them feature that one on *Dancing with the Stars*. What's it called, the 'Crackyourknackerena'? I hope that one makes it into a movie that stars Kevin Bacon – who wouldn't want to see *Cockloose*?

'Drunk driver caught having sex while driving'. I guess it was the second time that night someone had asked him to 'blow into this'.

'Female virgin sells virginity online for $20,000'. In other news, male virgin posts blog about new *Star Trek* film online.

'Sex theme park in China closes down'. Apparently no man could find the small information booth entrance, and blokes kept trying to sneak in the back.

'Couple caught having sex on Queen's lawn'. I guess that's at Her Majesty's Pleasure. I wonder if they did it corgi-style.

'Star of *Gilmore Girls* makes a porno'. Will they call it 'Fill-more Girls'?

Speaking of porn (and that's not an expression you get to use all the time) who could forget this one: 'University uses porn as alternative to drinking binges'. Are they calling the initiative 'spit don't swallow'?

While we're on the subject of knobs, political headlines are also often much more interesting than the words that follow. Like the news that 'Publisher releases special edition of Costello memoirs'. I'm guessing it's special because, like Pete himself, it has no spine.

And I couldn't go past this header: 'Turnbull says unemployment figures will rise again'. Yes, most likely when he loses his job. Then there's the poor leader of the Greens:

SOMETHING OLD, SOMETHING NEW...

'Brown to lose seat for being bankrupt'. I felt sorry for Bob when it looked like he might lose his Senate position; but when he thought about the morally or ethically bankrupt politicians around him, perhaps he didn't feel too bad.

And then of course there was the trouble with Telstra. 'Telstra appoints new CEO' blared the headline. Sadly, immediately afterwards the CEO went into a tunnel and dropped out.

'Trujillo calls Australia racist'. Okay, Sol might have a point there. After all, we do have a show called *Spicks and Specks*. On the other hand, we're not the ones getting sick from pashing pigs.

When it comes to politics, there's one headline I wish I'd seen this year. With rumours of budget cuts to funding for the mentally ill, I really wanted to see the papers run with: 'The pain from Wayne falls mainly on insane!'

Perhaps my love of words and puns stems from my childhood growing up on a farm very close to a timber town. Before I go any further: for those fancy big-city folk who don't know what I'm talking about, this doesn't mean it was located between a straw town and a brick town and was regularly threatened by wolves. No, it means that the main source of employment in the area came from the local sawmill, so occasionally upon meeting someone you'd just shake hands, and if they really liked you, you'd get a high-three.

It was the sort of town where, if someone wanted to give you the finger, they would actually give you one of their fingers. Most football presentation nights were more like Buddhist ceremonies filled with the sound of one hand clapping.

I was particularly fascinated by the stories behind people's nicknames. Being the bush, there were a lot of opposites: a big boofy bloke called Tiny, a blood-nut called Blue, and a whole bunch of tiny blue people . . . oh hang on, I think I'm getting confused with The Smurfs.

But there were also other crackers. One bloke in town was called Kit-Kat because he only had four fingers; there was Showbag because he was full of crap; and my absolute favourite, this old fella called Clock, who was one of the best footy players in town despite one of his hands sporting only two fingers. After playing football alongside him for about two years, I finally got up the courage to ask why everyone called him Clock. He smiled and said, 'Mate, because I've got one big hand and one little hand, of course.'

Australians are world-famous for their nicknames – but there is one rule: you can't choose it yourself. I guess this is to prevent every second Aussie bloke calling himself Hung-Like-a-Horse Hamilton (although with our penchant for opposite nicknames, maybe that wouldn't be so good after all).

A few years ago I had the good fortune to interview one of my heroes, best-selling British author Neil Gaiman. I asked him if he had a nickname when he was growing up, and he laughed and said, 'No . . . but then again I didn't grow up in Australia.'

Personally, I think he should be grateful he didn't go to school here; with a name that sounds like Kneel Gay Man, kids' heads would have exploded.

FIVE

AUSSIE AUSSIE AUSSIE, EH EH EH

I love Australia. I couldn't be more Aussie if I was riding a kangaroo down the street, eating a Vegemite sandwich, drinking a VB and staring at a picture of Boonie – all while dressed as Alf Stewart from *Home and Away*.

I'm Aussie as. Could not be Aussier if. But, at the risk of sounding like a flamin' un-Australian mongrel, there is not a term I hate more in our vernacular than 'un-Australian'.

Now to some readers that will automatically label me as a long-haired, dole-bludging, chardonnay-sipping, tree-shagging, flag-burning, feminazi, lezbollah, latte leftie member of the inner-city elite, who doesn't know what it's like for the silent majority of LABs (Little Aussie Battlers) who live on, or a short cab ride from, Struggle Street.

And I must confess they're right. I don't know what it's like. After all, the only people who *truly* know what it's like to be a battler are millionaire right-wing talkback hosts. They know battlers because they employ many of them as their butlers.

But to me, the term 'un-Australian' is the cane toad of our language and it continues to spread. At this rate, next year we won't celebrate Australia Day, we'll have un-Australian Day. Politicians and talkback radio hosts will crown the un-Australian of the Year while a choir sing the anthem 'Advance Australia Unfair' and then chant 'Aussie Aussie Aussie! Noi Noi Noi!' (All this, of course, will be faithfully reported in the *un-Australian* newspaper.)

So what exactly is it about the dreaded label that I find so offensive? Well, for starters, it's so insular. Why, in the amazing international community we're part of, do we feel the need to define ourselves so narrowly? What's next? Un-Victorian? Un-Rooty-Hillian? I mean, how small do we want to go?

'Excuse me, it says here you've lived in this city for twenty years and yet you've never killed someone in a really bizarre fashion; that's totally un-Adeladian!'

Or: 'G'day mate, I see you have three kids and none of them have mullets. That's totally un-Townsvillian!'

Or even: 'You mean you've never smoked, got drunk, got fat, taken drugs, taken money from a bookie or shagged around? That's totally un-Shane Warnian!'

Which leads me to my second problem: what we choose to label un-Australian. After all, when we locked children in the desert detention centres there was barely an un-Oz whisper to be heard, but when petrol hit $1.40 people in the street were chanting, 'Petrol is $1.40! That's un-Australian! The only way I can calm down is by drinking this $3 bottle of water and eating this $20 banana!'

I guess I just don't understand how we decide what is Australian and what is not. (With the possible exception of those who watch the Ashes and say, 'I wish the Poms could have made it more of a contest!' Even I agree that is un-Australian.) Surely, by its very definition, it is Aussie to do whatever Aussies do. 'What's that mate? You went to Bali and you didn't smuggle drugs? Well, that is un-Australian!'

I think it shows a real lack of clear identity that we constantly define ourselves by what we aren't. When I fill in a form that asks for my sex I write 'male' I don't write 'un-girly'. Firstly, because it would be stupid, and secondly, because it would be a lie. I'm, like, totally girly.

It seems to me that as a nation we're afraid to admit that Australians are just like everyone else. We're good, bad, smart, stupid, brave, cowardly, grumpy, dopey, sneezy and Doc. (OK, you got me. I ran out of ideas at the end there and just started naming dwarves.) Instead, we seem to think that if something is worthy of praise it is immediately Australian; and conversely, if it's bad it's un-Australian. For example, when Russell Crowe won his Academy Award he was a top Aussie, but when he threw the phone he was suddenly from New Zealand.

And sadly, calling someone un-Australian seems to be a trait that, well, is particularly Australian. After all, you don't really hear about people being described as un-Swiss, un-Greenlandish or even un-Iraqi.

I mean, are the people of Kyrgyzstan currently having a national debate on un-Kyrgyzstani behaviour? And what exactly would that consist of, other than not being particularly landlocked and using too many vowels in the spelling of place names?

Are people who walk into a bar but aren't amusing accused of being un-Irish? Are those who are really good at cricket labelled un-English? Are women with hairy bikini-lines being called un-Brazilian? And what if a backpacker to this country gets a job; will that make them an un-New Zealander?

Ah, yes, taking the puss out of Kiwis, now that is truly Australian. Just to prove what a patriot I am, let me tell you about my trip to the Land of the Long White Cloud.

I was in the country to perform for the first time at the New Zealand Comedy Festival, so as I bounced off the plane I must admit I was a bundle of nerves. My anxiety only increased when I jumped into the front seat of a cab. In the driver's seat was big burly bloke sporting what looked less like a beard and more like I had interrupted him halfway through eating a live sheep.

He turned to me and barked, 'Your first time in New Zealand bro?'

I explained that it was my second visit, and that I had lived in Bondi for five years so I was used to being surrounded by Kiwis. 'It's nice to finally meet one who has a job though,' I joked.

It seemed I had accidentally grabbed a big can marked 'worms' and a tin-opener.

'Don't talk to me about bloody Aussies, bro,' he said. 'Mean country. Refugees float through the ocean on boats, they get to your country and you tell them to go away, but we ... we take them in!'

Now, I'm no defender of Australia's once hardline policy on asylum-seekers, but I quipped, 'Well, you need them, don't you? You have to replace all the New Zealanders who have moved to Australia.'

Deafening silence. The sort of silence you can hear. Finally punctured by him asking, 'Do you know who invented bungee-jumping?'

'Um, someone who was sick of their dad saying, "If your best friend jumped off a bridge, would you?"'

He ignored me. 'It was a New Zealander!'

'Impressive,' I said, not actually impressed at all.

'You know a New Zealander also invented jogging,' he continued.

I chuckled slightly, assuming he was joking, but the look on his face told me he was deadly serious.

'Bu ... bu ... but surely people have jogged since the beginning of time, right?' I stammered. 'I mean, I'm pretty sure the first person to have a large angry animal run towards them probably invented jogging ... and sprinting ... and swearing, I imagine?'

'No,' he said, having none of my flawless argument, 'it was invented by a New Zealander. A bloke called Arthur Lydiard invented jogging as a method of keeping fit.'

I was about to ask if he was pulling my leg, but thought better of it, as I feared it might lead to an entire conversation about a bloke from Dunedin inventing leg-pulling. Instead I countered with, 'So what you're really saying is he named jogging, aren't you?'

All I heard from under his beard was a grunt, which I took as meaning either, 'I see your point and I will think on it and get back to you at another time' or, 'I know places I could bury you where they will never find the body.'

We both decided it was time to move on. I started to fumble with my phone as a distraction, but he ignored the hint.

'Did you know New Zealand is part of the Pacific rim of fire?' he continued.

No, I did not. In fact I didn't (and still don't) know what that is. It sounded to me like the side-effect of a particularly spicy curry.

I put my phone to my ear, pretending it had rung, to break the awkwardness.

'Did you know you can get your driver's licence at fifteen in New Zealand?' he asked.

I put my phone down. 'Wow,' I breathed, as it seemed to be the reaction he was seeking, and to be honest he was starting to scare me slightly. 'I guess that means when you see a "Baby on Board" sticker they might be talking about the driver.'

Nothing.

'Did you know that New Zealand is the youngest country in the entire world?' he beamed.

'I did not,' I admitted. 'But it does explain why it occasionally has to borrow some fake ID and pretend it's Australia.'

Nothing.

'Do you know why they call us the Land of the Long White Cloud?' he asked.

'No,' I replied again, 'but it must make reporting the weather easy. Today, cloudy again!'

Nothing.

'Did you know in the 1900s in New Zealand there were twenty sheep to every person, but now the ratio is only nine to one?'

I knew it was probably time to bite my tongue, but I couldn't resist: 'Maybe they all just shaved their fleece into mullets and moved to Australia? In fact, perhaps that's why Kiwi blokes say "choice" all the time. They miss the days when they had some.'

Tumbleweeds.

It was at this point that my cabbie really started to frighten me. He moved closer and whispered slightly more aggressively than I would have expected, 'Do you pee?'

I was slightly freaked out. Was he going to ask for a sample? Because if he continued in this manner there might have been one on the floor of his cab. I nodded nervously.

'You shouldn't do it,' he snapped. 'We have a big problem with pee in this country!'

What the? Did he expect me to hold on? And what was their big problem? Kiwi blokes' bad aim? Too much asparagus? Willie Mason?

Finally the cab driver seemed to realise my confusion and explained that P (rather than pee) was a drug that was causing many problems in New Zealand society.

I tried to laugh off my mistake: 'P? Wow, I have been out of the loop. I stopped at E. I didn't know they'd kept going. I'd like to try some Q!'

Nothing.

He went on to explain that P is the local term for crystal meth – what we would call ice. (Although to be honest, I'm not sure why Kiwis would take a drug to keep you awake. I mean, there's not that much to do there, and you can only watch *Lord of the Rings* so many times.)

At last we seemed to be bonding, and yet for some reason I felt my lips continue to move. 'Well, of course people like to get high in this country,' I said. 'It's the home of Sir Edmund Hillary and he got higher than anyone in the world. Although I guess when most people get high they don't take a Sherpa along for company, do they?'

The air was suddenly thinner and colder than it is on Mount Everest; but like Hillary, I felt the need to push on despite the danger. 'Do you know why he had to climb Everest?' I asked.

He grunted at me angrily, but I was unstoppable now. 'It was the only place on the planet where people wouldn't mock him for having a girl's name.'

I could tell I was starting to get a reaction of sorts. He looked at me and said, 'You know he climbed it again, don't you?'

'Yes,' I replied. 'But he had to. A lot of people don't know this, but he left his wallet up there with his Video Ezy card inside.'

Tough crowd.

As he started another rant about the country being ruined by too many teenagers smoking pot, we finally pulled up at my hotel. I opened the door, grabbed my bags, threw some money on the seat and tried one last time. 'Well, maybe that's why they call it the Land of the Long White Cloud!'

News of my credentials as a true-blue, Kiwi-mocking Aussie must have travelled the globe, because when I landed in London a few months later, I found myself on the news.

Now before you start making assumptions – no, I didn't try to take in a boogie-board bag full of Schapelle's secret stash, touch up the Queen Paul Keating-style or spend a night in a hotel room with Gordon Ramsay.

No, I was on the news defending our country. Why me, you ask? Well, apart from the aforementioned credentials, all I can guess is it must have been one of those rare occasions when Kevin Rudd was actually in Australia (visiting from his backpacking tour of Europe), so they checked which Aussies were in town, saw Jason Donovan and Dannii Minogue, and figured I was the best of a bad bunch.

But the reason *why* I was asked to defend our beautiful home GBS (girt by sea) is far more interesting. As it turned out, the English had taken particular exception to an advertisement put out by the Australian Sports Commission. The story was making front-page news in the tabloid press (whose motto, incidentally, seems to be 'Small Words, Big Type, Bigger Boobs').

And suddenly I was an expert. Yes, it turns out that all it takes to be an expert is a mixture of being 'convenient' and 'cheap'.

Now, if you haven't seen the ad I'm talking about, it was a viral email starring a boasting Brit that was meant to arouse anger and passion in Aussies. (As opposed to being angry about picking up something viral from a British backpacker after a night of passion.) If you can't be bothered looking it up on YouTube, it stars an actor – with a less-convincing British accent than Madonna – taunting Australia about our Olympic gold medal count. Why the ad agency couldn't find an actual geezer for the ad, I don't know. Surely they could have just popped down to Bondi Beach and asked every second person? Or lured them with a free chip?

Anyway, I found myself on national television in the UK, the cameras in my face, the lights burning in my eyes, being asked: 'Would it work?'

I had to confess, maybe. (Oh yeah, they were really getting their money's worth with my outrageous opinions.) Maybe.

You see, even though the ad makes Rob Schneider's *Big Stan* look like a work of comedic genius, I do think the sentiment behind it rings true. Or true-ish. (By this stage I was starting to realise I was going to get splinters if I sat on the fence any longer!)

True-ish.

I reckon most Australians would confess that in certain areas we've always seen ourselves as superior to the Brits – weather and dentistry are a couple that spring immediately to mind. But sporting prowess is the one that trumps them all. Sometimes I suspect we'd be happy to come second-last in the medal count at the Olympics, as long as Great Britain came last. (Well actually, probably third-last, because we'd want to make sure we beat New Zealand too.)

In most countries the Olympic motto is *Citius, Altius, Fortius*, but in Australia it is *Citius, Altius, Fortius, Beatius Pommius Bastardus*.

And as much as the Olympics should be about celebrating the spirit of taking part and striving for excellence, it genuinely did a) surprise us, and b) burn us up that the Brits beat us.

Remember when it happened? It basically knocked all other news off the front page. Suddenly no-one cared about terrorism. Forget beat the bombs, it was all about being beaten by the Poms.

And beaten we were. Every mathematician in the country was pulled off important research to prove that we won more medals 'per capita' than Great Britain. (Of course, going on that logic, the most successful country in the world was Michael Phelpistan). Then we decided that even though the British total was nineteen gold to our fourteen, six of those medals were won by the Welsh and the Scottish so they didn't count.

Hell, if the Poms could compete as Great Britain, we should combine with other countries too . . . maybe we could be the United States of Australia, or Chinalia?

We just couldn't admit that the British had beaten us fair and square. Put it this way, if they'd awarded a gold medal for coming up with excuses and justifications, we certainly could have added that one to the list.

'So where does this rivalry come from?' I was asked.

Well, my theory is that we resent the British because they think we're convicts, and they resent us because someone stole a loaf of bread in cold, wet, plague-riddled London and they sent them to Summer Bay. (After landing in Sydney Harbour, I bet the convicts started sending excited messages home: 'Next time steal two loaves of bread; they might send you on a Kontiki cruise to Tahiti!')

The other reason we like to play this game is simply that sporting rivalries are mostly harmless and fun.

After the Olympics, our sports minister Kate Ellis had to wear a British tracksuit because she'd lost a bet over which country would win the most gold medals. Which got me thinking, maybe we were too hard on John Howard for all those years over his trackies; maybe he just kept losing bets.

That's part of the joy of sport. I mean, you can't imagine having to do that in any other portfolio, can you? You can't imagine defence ministers having a bet whereby the army that shoots the least people has to wear the other team's uniform into combat?

And that's what's worth remembering: it's the Olympics, it's not a matter of life and death. But most importantly, we shouldn't let it distract us from what really matters . . . the Ashes.

Barracking for the Australian cricket team brings rich rewards — not least victory, and the chance to lord it over the Poms. But most importantly for me, it makes a refreshing change from barracking for the Western Bulldogs, a team that can't even spell the word 'victory'.

Yes, dear readers, for some people September is a happy time. Spring has sprung, the flowers are blooming, the weather is improving and so are people's moods. Well, everyone's, that is, except mine. I hate September.

Now, I don't want to come across all Grinchy McGrinch, but at last count I've had 35 Septembers in my life and have hated every single one, without exception. In fact, I'm not sure 'hate' is a strong enough word. Perhaps 'abhor' is more appropriate. Or 'despise', 'detest', 'execrate' or 'loathe'. (No, I didn't consult a thesaurus: I just looked up the terms people used to describe Kyle Sandilands on the *Idol* blogs.)

You know how some hotels don't have a thirteenth floor due to superstition? (Although who are they kidding? Floor fourteen knows what it really is.) Well, if I designed calendars there would be no September.

Clearly this would piss off a lot of Virgos (firstly, because they would miss their birthday, but mostly because they would have less time to clean and organise things), but it would certainly make my life more pleasant.

Folks, if I could, I would go to bed on 31 August and not wake up until 1 October. Come the last day of August, I cruise bars hoping someone will slip Rohypnol in my drink. So why do I want to go all Rip Van Winkle on September, I hear you ask? What could possibly make me hate a simple month so much? You guessed it: footy finals.

Now, I don't mean to imply I don't love my football team. I do. They are, in fact, my greatest passion. Most people's blood has only red and white blood cells; mine has blue as well.

When they win I feel so happy that I imagine smiley faces on T-shirts are pictures of me, and when they lose even emo kids think I am too depressed. And therein lies the rub. Because in all my thirty-five years I have never seen the Doggies play in a grand final, let alone win one. For some clubs, September is a time of hopes and dreams; for the Bulldogs it's a time of disappointments and planning end-of-season trips. I don't know what I did in a previous life to deserve this, but I assume I must have driven a truck full of black cats under a row of ladders and then crashed it into a mirror factory.

Barracking for the Western Bulldogs is like having an ugly baby: you know everyone else reckons it should have a paper bag over its head, but you think it's beautiful. Or at least that's what you tell yourself.

For those who don't follow footy, I'll give you the CliffsNotes. The Western Bulldogs were originally called Footscray, but changed their name after they informed on a mob boss and had to go into the Witness Relocation Program. OK, I may have made that last bit up. They have only ever played in two grand finals: they won one in 1954 (twenty years before I was born) and lost one in 1961 (thirteen years before I was born). I guess on the upside, we're saving a lot on silver polish.

But just pause and think about that for a moment. The last time my club won a flag was in 1954. 1954. To put this in perspective, if I had been around then and missed the game I wouldn't have been able to catch the replay because ... Australia didn't have television!

When my team last won a flag, the average price of a car was $1200; these days that's about what it costs to fill up a tank. Forget the Sydney Olympics, when the Doggies last got to sing their theme song on the final weekend in September, people were still looking forward to the Melbourne Games.

These days Aboriginal players dominate the AFL; when my team last won a premiership they weren't even allowed to vote!

I've heard some fans talk about the pain of seeing their team lose on grand final day. I'd just like to see my team *on the ground* on grand final day. These days I'd probably settle for them singing with the *Idol* finalists during the half-time entertainment.

Some clubs expect success; you only have to listen to their theme songs to hear it. The Hawks, for example, sing, 'We're a happy team at Hawthorn.' But if you're a Doggies' fan, it's more like, 'We're an occasionally happy team, but to be honest, disappointed most of the time.' After victories, the Cats sing, 'We are Geelong, the greatest team of all.' Well, down the road in the western suburbs it's usually more like, 'We are the dogs, we're just glad to make the eight!'

On the other hand, if you barrack for the Bulldogs you know you don't do it for silverware and bragging rights; you are doing it out of loyalty and love.

And being a Doggies' fan certainly means that you are well-prepared for setbacks and disappointments in life. Hell, I can be watching a replay of a game I *know* they won and still expect them to find some way to lose.

And yet.

And yet. Every year, there it is again. That little tingle in my stomach. No, not gas . . . hope. Hope that one day, September might become my favourite month of the year. You see, for all the pain and heartbreak they've caused me over the years, I truly wouldn't swap my beloved Doggies for all the other clubs' Premiership cups combined. After all, as every footy fan will tell you: there's always next year.

Still, even my best attempts at optimism occasionally fail me, and I have to resort to reliving past glories in order to cheer myself up. The other day I found myself reminiscing about the magnificent career of one of our most impressive champions: Ian Thorpe. Wiping a tear from my eye, I decided to pen him a letter . . .

Dear Ian, aka Thorpey, the Thorpedo, Thorpey McThorpe, the Super-Duper Fish,

Like most Aussies, I am still a little sad that you decided to retire from swimming. But remembering the look on your face at your final press conference, I'm slowly beginning to accept that Phar Lap has more chance of making a comeback than you do. And thinking back on your announcement, I thought you conducted yourself with real class. If it had been me, I would have got Craig Stevens to do it.

It was especially great to hear you talk with pride about your career – and what a stellar career it was. Five Olympic gold medals and ten at the Commonwealth Games. Wow, the only time I've won anything was on the clowns at the Heyfield Timber Festival, and even then it was only a large foam hand that said 'No Fat Chicks'.

But that's not all. From 1999 to 2002, you broke thirteen world records. The only time I have broken that many was when I discovered a mate had put The Best of Nickelback *in my vinyl collection. I find it amazing that you started breaking records when you were only fifteen. When I was that age, I couldn't scratch my arse without a set of instructions from my* mother. (And I was certainly too afraid to get into a pair of Speedos, in case I saw a cute girl and suddenly developed a certain winged keel.)

Sure, there are some people who think you retired too early, but I can't believe you kept at it for so long. If I were you and my alarm went off at 4.17 am, I would have thought, 'Hmmm, should I get up and swim lap after lap, or should I sleep in and then get up and roll around in my cash?'

I read somewhere that you'd swim three hundred laps a day, or about fifteen kilometres. Wow, double wow. Most of us would get puffed driving fifteen kilometres. Some days I find it too much of a hassle to have a bath.

What else did you have to achieve? You already have more gold than Rose Hancock on a date with Mr T. If you wore all your medals at the same time, you'd look like a poker machine paying out.

Now, I know there are a few journos who've given you a hard time for going to LA, but so what if you want to hang out with Hollywood stars? If I'd known it might have led to meeting Scarlett Johansson, I would've tried a lot harder at swimming in high school (and I'd be a much better breast-stroker by now).

Anyway, you don't have to worry about all that any more. For years, your body was a temple, so now I hope you're treating it like an amusement park. You know how they say you shouldn't go swimming within half an hour of eating? Well, I suggest you have a feed every twenty-five minutes for the next two years.

The only time you should go near a pool is to fill it with jelly crystals so you can eat your way to the other end. You should put your head so far into a bucket of chicken it would look like you're impersonating Ned Kelly.

You should replace all your gold medals with chocolate coins and chow down until your bodysuit needs a girdle and the only sponsor you can get is Goodyear. If you still want to compete, you could enter one of those crappy Japanese contests to see how fast you can eat hotdogs. (That's the fast food I'm talking about, not the host of that crappy Up-Late Game Show.*)*

Anyway, congratulations again on a wonderful career and thanks for all the joy you brought me over the years. Sure, it wasn't always smooth sailing. There was the time at the Olympic trials when you did a dive so bad I thought you were an Italian soccer player; when you had to pull out of the Commonwealth Games because you were 'fully sick'; and I have to confess I sometimes thought the fashion was a bit Thorpe Eye for the Sports Guy.

But I think it's really admirable that, unlike some people (you know who I'm talking about Shane Warne), you were always a great role-model for kids. (Although I guess it's a lot harder to use your mobile phone underwater, and you'd have to swim backstroke to keep your smokes dry.)

So, I hope you're happy and enjoying life. If you're bored and looking for a television gig, I know the ABC has a spare slot on a Wednesday. Maybe it's time for a new, edgier Undercover Angels*?*

Or, because you're amazingly well-spoken, smart and loved by Australians, perhaps you should think about joining the Liberals. It's no secret they need you.
Cheers, Wil

It's true about the Liberals — with Kyoto signed, 'sorry' said, and WorkChoices fired, that team seems to be in a policy vacuum. Since I was in the mood for dispensing advice, I spent the rest of the afternoon thinking up some policy suggestions for Malcolm Turnbull and the Liberal Party that might win them some votes.

How about this one? We all agree that the government needs traffic fines to raise revenue, so what about fining people for other, more annoying, offences? I think motorists would vote for Turnbull if he promised on-the-spot fines for people who pick their nose at traffic lights, or speed cameras that issue fines to people in the right-hand lane who travel *under* the speed limit.

However, while I appreciate that fines and taxes are an important part of the government's revenue, they do cause resentment in the community. So what about this for a policy? Mr Turnbull could promise that every time someone received a tax bill or fine from the government, it would be accompanied by a voucher for a Golden Gaytime. That way their anger at the bill would be offset by enjoying a delicious ice-cream.

Politicians often talk about zero tolerance against crime, but I'd like to bring in zero tolerance against annoying people.

How about an electric charge fitted to elevator buttons and pedestrian buttons at traffic lights, so if you have pushed the button and then someone else pushes it again, they get a shock?

Kevin Rudd talks about his education revolution, but I reckon Malcolm Turnbull could win some votes simply by promising to concentrate on the little things.

How about a policy that by the year 2020, no child in the country will say 'brought' when they actually mean 'bought' or 'aks' when they mean 'ask'? And I am usually completely against the death penalty, but Mr Turnbull could win my vote by promising the electric chair for anyone who says 'anythink' instead of 'anything'. Seriously, there is somethink wrong with these people!

While I am on the topic, could we also ban anyone saying 'ATM machine'? As the 'M' stands for 'machine', they are actually saying 'Automatic Teller Machine machine'. And 'tuna fish' — after all, you wouldn't ask for a 'steak cow mammal sandwich', would you?

One of the criticisms being levelled at the Libs is that they are not in touch with kids, so here's a new technology policy for Mr Turnbull: no-one should be able to use the acronyms 'LOL' or 'ROFL' in a text message or email unless they are in fact 'laughing out loud' or 'rolling on the floor laughing'.

And finally, if there is one thing Aussies love, it's days off. If Malcolm really wants to win back some votes, he should make the last weekend of every month a long weekend. In addition to the Queen's Birthday long weekend, let's have Prince Charles's Birthday, Prince Philip's Birthday, Prince William's Birthday and Prince-Harry-Bought-a-New-Bong Day off as well.

Plus, most states already have a Labor Day public holiday: why not balance the ledger with a Liberal Day? And maybe throw in a National Party Day, too, and make it a four-day weekend? Actually, while we're at it, most Aussies tend to clock off work at about lunchtime on Friday anyway, so why not make it official? Screw Kyoto, Malcolm would definitely steal some votes off Kev if he promised a two-and-a-half day weekend.

But the reform that is long overdue is making the Melbourne Cup – the race that truly does stop the nation – a public holiday for the whole country. If we really want to be flamin' fair dinkum in the fight against al-Qaeda, it's the very least we can do.

No-one can argue that there isn't something really special about the Melbourne Cup. If nothing else, it's the only time usually rational people set their alarms early on a day off, then spend hours fighting traffic just to sit in a car park getting pissed. It's like going to the movies but, instead of going inside the cinema, spending the entire time sculling Coke and snorting lines of Wizz Fizz at the candy bar.

That said, a part of me thinks you could get one of your mates to dress in a gorilla suit and another to wear a tux jacket with boardies while drinking VB out of your boot at the local Westfield car park and save yourself the drive.

The current situation in places outside of Melbourne is that people get to stop work for the duration of the race. So if the whole day isn't declared a public holiday, at the very least they should have the decency to make the race longer. Forget five minutes, get the horses to run a marathon – that way we'd get a couple of hours off. Or make it like Bathurst, or even better, like *The Amazing Race*.

Yes, get the horses to visit twelve different countries and complete a series of difficult challenges. Sure, it's pretty exciting now, but imagine how much cooler it would be to see a horse bungee-jump!

I do love the races. I love horses, I love the trainers, I love the bookies and in particular, I love the jockeys. Although I don't like it when they whip the horses to make them run faster, partly because I think it's cruel, and partly because at the clubs I go to you have to pay extra for that.

And I don't think it's right that the winner gets a cup. I mean, how can horses hold up a cup with their hooves? Surely they should compete for something they'll appreciate, like the Melbourne Apple, the Melbourne Cube of Sugar, or the Melbourne DVD Box Set of *Mister Ed*?

But why do we make such a big deal about the jockeys' weight when the horses are then given extra weight in their saddlebags? Why can't we just have fat jockeys? Wouldn't it be great to see a jumbo jockey squeezed into his silks, trying to negotiate the course at Flemington while simultaneously eating a bucket of chicken?

Without a doubt, the thing I love most about jockeys is their voices. There are always plenty of rumours about drugs in racing, but I think they should investigate whether the jockeys are inhaling helium in order to be lighter in the saddle. If nothing else, it would explain the way they talk. Seriously folks, some of their voices are so high they make Beaker from *The Muppet Show* sound like the son of Barry White and Peter Harvey, Canberra.

And is there anything more entertaining than that bloke trying to do the post-race interviews on the back of his horse? I think all interviews should be done like that. I'd love to see Kerry O'Brien chase the Prime Minister around Parliament House on a horse, or Tracy Grimshaw canter down the street on a Shetland pony after a dodgy washing-machine repairman.

Still, let's be honest here folks, the horses and jockeys are only the supporting players. The real action is off the track – Flemington becomes a giant version of a Desperate and Dateless Ball. You do have to watch your alcohol intake, though. One year I had too many shandies and woke up with a horse in my bed. For a moment I thought the Mafia had put out a hit on me.

By the way, if you're curious about those hospitality marquees, I believe the most exclusive are Emirates, Moët & Chandon and Myer. I would love to tell you what they're like, but unfortunately I only ever get invited to Bi-Lo, Crazy Clark's and Not Quite Right.

For the ladies, of course, it's all about the hats – and the bigger the better. It's the only day of the year when Molly Meldrum looks underdressed. But I am not a fan of the fascinator. To me it sounds like a B-grade Arnie movie: 'I'll be back . . . and I'll look fabulous!'

Whatever your area of interest, the race is always a cracker. In fact, even if you don't live in Melbourne you should take the day off. Go on, do it for yourself, do it for Australia. If you don't, the terrorists have already won.

Speaking of terrorists, I have a rather embarrassing confession to make: I'm completely bored with the whole terrorism thing. I know I shouldn't be – I've read the papers and still have those fridge magnets. But try as I might to be alert and not alarmed, the closest I can get is tired and emotional, irritable and restless, drunk and giggly – or most of the time, just plain hungry.

I realise I should be more worried about the Impending Threat of Terrorism and the War on Terror (and other things I know are important because they spell them in capital letters in the paper), but to be honest most of the time I'm more anxious about the fact that if I don't start a diet soon, the only use for my belt will be as a support bra for my man boobs. On my 'things that are likely to kill me' list, terrorism comes well below such dangers as eating fatty foods, drinking too much, lack of exercise and Shannon Noll.

In fact, when you start to consider the various ways you can cark it, terrorism ranks fairly low and you have to wonder what all the fuss is about. For example, in the same year that 3000 people died in the 9/11 attacks, 300,000 people died in America from obesity-related illnesses.

Perhaps we should stop worrying about Iran's weapons of mass destruction and worry more about Whoppers of Mass Destruction. Maybe the true axis of evil is McDonald's, KFC and Krispy Kreme.

Maybe, just maybe, we should spend a little less time looking for Osama and his secret plans for world destruction, and concentrate instead on the Colonel and his eleven secret herbs and spices.

The truth is, sometimes the hysteria around a particular threat outweighs the actual danger it poses. In the weeks after 9/11, more people died from car crashes because they were afraid to get on a plane than they did in the actual attacks. And to put that in perspective, the roads were much safer back then, because Lindsay Lohan didn't have her driver's licence.

Don't you dare pat a dog, either, because statistically, you're four times more likely to die of a dog bite than a terrorist attack. Forget terrorism ad campaigns, the government should send out more 'Beware of the Dog' stickers. Forget the War on Terror, we need a War on Terriers. Forget al-Qaeda, Alsatians are the real threat to our way of life.

Even things we do every day without the slightest worry are more likely to cause our death than terrorism. For example, more people die in Australia from injuries sustained while kicking buckets than in terrorist attacks. OK, I made that one up.

But you are eight times more likely to die falling from a ladder than from terrorism. Eight times! Where the bloody hell is my fridge magnet about that? Eight times more likely – and that doesn't count being hit by a terrorist plane while on a ladder. We shouldn't have invaded Iraq, we should have invaded Bunnings.

If you really want to be safe, opt to take showers – more people drown in bathtubs in the US every year than die of terrorism worldwide. (Obviously this is less of a problem in Britain, because they hardly ever take baths.) Yes, move over Anthrax, it's Radox that should really concern us. Forget Ban the Bomb, maybe we should Ban the Bath. It would save lives while also helping with the water restrictions. At the very least we should set up metal detectors. After all, people aren't allowed to take nail-clippers on planes, but they're using them in the tub without a thought to the horrible consequences.

And that's not all. You are also ten times more likely to die being struck by lightning than by a terrorist attack. And Steven Jacobs doesn't warn you about terrorist attacks on the long-range forecast on the *Today* show weather. So it's a lot more risky playing golf in the rain than it is catching a plane. Especially if you also happen to be holding an umbrella and wearing a tin-foil hat.

And then, of course, there are the select group of people who will fall off a ladder after being struck by lightning and then drown in the tub where they were bathing their dog. But for me, the statistic that puts it all in perspective is this: you are twice as likely to die from being crushed under a vending machine than you are to meet your maker as a result of a terror attack. (I have to confess, a part of me believes that if you are crushed under a vending machine it's not a tragedy, it's natural selection. Of all the ways to go, it's not exactly the most glamorous, is it?)

So it seems to me that there are many more things we need to be alert and alarmed about; and top of my list at the moment is the appalling level of service offered by Telstra.

Seriously folks, I knew I had to do something about my phone when a mate called me from the Serengeti recently and the line dropped out at my end.

According to the ads, Telstra is meant to have about 98 percent coverage in this country. If this is true, the other 2 percent must be between my lounge room and my kitchen. So the other week I finally bit the bullet, climbed into the cupboard under the sink where the reception is actually pretty clear, and gave Telstra a call. An hour and a half later I was still on hold.

An hour and a half! Don't these organisations realise that most people have better things to do with their time than be kept on hold? I mean I don't, but I'm sure people with real jobs do.

And while we're on the topic, let's talk about the hold music — and by that I don't mean the mix tape of mood-tunes Warnie puts on when he's about to make a special phone call. The music they play is ridiculous. I could understand if it was 'Ring Ring' or 'Hanging on the Telephone', but all you hear over and over is that bloody 'I Am Australian' song. After about the fifteenth time hearing that 'we are one but we are many', you can't help but have some very, very un-Australian thoughts.

I'm beginning to suspect that most terrorist acts in this country aren't caused by religious or racial differences after all; it's the anger from being left on hold at Telstra for too long. At one point I was tempted — when I finally got through — to ask for the number of someone who could supply me with fertiliser, electrical equipment and directions to Telstra's head office. Maybe David Hicks didn't want to join al-Qaeda at all. Maybe he was just trying to get broadband at his house in Adelaide when he decided to join the Taliban. (He mistakenly thought they were fighting for a 'telephone ban'.)

Even worse is when they interrupt the endless repeats of 'I Am Australian' to remind you about their 'fantastic products and services'. Really? Are any of these products and services related to the service of actually answering the phone? Because that *would* be fantastic. Telstra breaking in from hold music to remind you how good their service is, is like Ivan Milat pausing for a moment while stabbing you to remark on the sharpness of his knives.

If you're going to keep me hanging on for so long, at least tell me something useful. Keep me up-to-date with Brad and Angelina (are they on again, or off again? I have trouble keeping up) or, since we have plenty of time, explain what's happening on *Lost*.

Isn't there something wrong in our society when the only time you get to speak to a representative from your phone company is when they call you, in the middle of dinner, from India? 'Yes, actually, I would like to talk to you about my long-distance service provider, thanks for asking. And I have a couple of other issues too hang on, I'll go and get my list!'

Of course the nonstop fun doesn't stop when you finally get through. First you get the option menu which, for some reason, never seems to contain the option you need. 'Um, do you have any specials?'

Then there's the computerised speech recognition software that has either been programmed by Mark Holden or the Swedish Chef from *The Muppet Show*. I used to get really frustrated with this, but now I play a new game where I pretend I'm interviewing Stephen Hawking: 'So Steve, whatever happened to your Theory of Everything?' 'I'm sorry, I do not understand.' Ha, I'm smarter than Stephen Hawking! (Like I said, I have a lot of spare time on my hands.)

But things became really difficult once I finally got through to a real person. For starters, before you can even proceed with your inquiry you have to answer a series of questions, each one more difficult than the last.

Truly, at one stage I thought I'd accidentally speed-dialled Andrew O'Keefe, especially when the bloke at the other end told me he could only access my account if I could name seven films starring Pauly Shore.

Forget the new citizenship test, when new immigrants arrive in our country just give them a prepaid mobile. If they can negotiate the security questions at Telstra then they deserve to be in.

Anyhoo, after I had given my address, birthdate, family tree, star sign, mother's maiden name, best mate's nickname, Snoop Dogg's real name, shoe size, inner-leg measurement, five favourite films, secret ingredient in my nanna's lasagne and DNA sample, I finally got through to the department I was looking for.

This is when I started to think I may have accidentally licked a cane-toad, because the lovely lady from Telstra – and I swear on the complete *Buffy* box set that this is true – said to me: 'We can't help you with that, we don't really deal with phones anymore!'

Okey and/or doke, let's go through that one more time so even the speech recognition software can understand it: 'We ...don't...really...deal...with...phones...anymore!'

Um, but aren't you Telstra? Isn't that what the 'tel' bit in your name stands for? Or are you just 'stra' now, like when Johnny Farnham went back to being John?

I was so stunned I even contemplated ringing the ACCC, but with the day I was having I was worried I'd spend three hours on hold, only to be told that they no longer deal with consumer complaints.

Since we're on the topic of dissatisfied customers, is it just me or are you starting to think that the best savings plan during the recession might be to hide your money under your mattress? Put it this way, you know you're in trouble when even the people who set the prices at airport food courts think the banks are greedy bastards.

If they're looking for material for sequels to *Underbelly*, then forget Carl Williams or the Lithgow mafia, they should go after the really big players fleecing innocent civilians of their hard-earned cash: the banks. 'Coming soon to Channel Nine, *Underbelly 3: A Tale of Two Tellers*. Who needs to sell guns and E's when you can make more money with overblown fees?'

Now, I know pointing out that banks charge outrageous fees is about as shocking as Anthony Callea revealing that he wasn't just waiting for the right girl to come along. But for me, the straw that broke the proverbial's back was all these new fees for using ATMs. These days when I put my card into an ATM, I half expect the Westpac lady who pops up on screen will be wearing a stocking over her head and pointing a gun. You know the fees are getting too high when you go down to the local RSL and end up losing more on the teller machine than on the pokies.

Now I don't deny anyone the right to charge for providing a service, but I also know when to call a spade a bloody rip-off. For the last few years, banks have done everything other than yell 'Fire!' to get us out of the branches so they can close them and maximise profits. Basically, we've been told our money is welcome to stay for as many sleepovers as it wants, but if we want to visit we'll have to do it from the street or our computers at home.

But here's the kicker: they want to charge us extra for the privilege of doing . . . it . . . ourselves.

I mean seriously, eat your heart out Bond villains. You can have all the laser guns and killer hats you want, this is true evil genius.

To put it in perspective, imagine you're hungry and want a pizza, so you ring up Dominos. They tell you that they don't deliver anymore. Oh well, you think, it's not that big a deal to go down to the shop and pick it up. But on the way you remember that they shut down your local Dominos last year, so you have to drive another ten minutes to the next one. Still, you have the hots for what's in the box with the dots, so you do.

Only here's the thing. When you get there, they haven't cooked the pizza for you, after all. No, they've just thrown some dough, cheese, tomatoes and anchovies in a box and you have to go home and make it yourself.

Here's the ultimate kicker: instead of giving you a discount for this, they charge you extra for the privilege. Genius. I'm just glad the banks don't control the sex industry; they'd probably charge you $250 per hour for do-it-yourself brothels.

And don't even start me on the exorbitant extras you have to pay if you use a rival's ATM. Sure, when you put your card in the slot you'll get told how much it's going to cost you, and you do have the option of pulling out . . . but while this may work for contraception in the Catholic Church, it's not great monetary policy.

In their defence, when the RBA relaxed the laws on ATM fees, the idea was to make the market more competitive and thus keep prices low. (Ah yes, the free market; and if you still believe that works, I have a Nigerian banking scheme I'll put you on to.) But instead of keeping fees down, they've just got higher . . . and higher . . . and higher. Who's the governor of the Reserve Bank these days? Larry Emdur?

ATM fees at some pubs are now higher than Pete Doherty, Amy Winehouse, Keith Richards and Cypress Hill doing a benefit concert for Michael Phelps at Nimbin.

Of course – as we are constantly told – if we don't like the fees we just have to shop around for a better deal. Sure, technically you can shop around, but sometimes there isn't a cheaper ATM nearby. I had to use one in a pub the other night and it cost me five bucks. Five bucks? I was only trying to get twenty out. That's a 25 percent charge – even my manager doesn't take that much. There are pimps out there who are charging more competitive rates.

If the ATM is going to charge me five bucks for the honour of accessing my own money, at the very least I should be able to put the transaction receipt in the front window of my car and get an hour's free parking.

And the idea of shopping around would make sense if there was actually any real choice; but let's be honest, choosing between the major banks is like choosing between the Daddos – no-one can tell them apart, and at the end of the day they're all as crap as each other.

I mean, if we needed any more proof, they're all starting to merge. Westpac and St George is now one superbank – which I guess is good news, as instead of having to go to two places to get shafted, you can now get shafted twice in the same place.

Although, if Westpac wanted to combine with another business, it should've merged with Bunnings. That way when they screw you, you'd be able to buy something to screw them back.

SIX
ROMANCING THE STONED

When it comes to fixing things around the house, it's fair to say I was never a handy man. At best, I was – or, more correctly, am – more of a dandy man or a have-the-occasional-shandy man. Forget *Backyard Blitz*, I'm a backyard ditz. If I produced that show it would be me and my mates coming around to your place while you were away and completely trashing it in under 24 hours.

When I was growing up I was never good at building stuff, and the only time I ever rubbed shoulders with people in overalls was when I went to a k.d lang concert. The only carpenters I knew were in my parents' record collection; the only time I'd used Selleys Liquid Nails was when I found some under the sink once and tried to ice a cake with it.

For most of my life I was the sort of person who is less DIY and more DIYTCAETRTD – Do It Yourself Then Call an Expert to Repair the Damage. (Even Jesus had better luck around wood and nails than I did.)

In the past the only thing I was handy at was picking up the phone to call hire-a-hubby. The fact is, I am a pretty hopeless joke of a bloke. Put it this way, you know you are in trouble when Thorpey thinks you're too metrosexual.

You don't believe me? Well, let's examine the evidence.

I put the toilet seat back down after I finish; I change my hairstyle more often than I change the oil and water in my car; and the only time I have ever worked with tools was when I was interviewed by Kyle Sandilands.

But wait, there's more. Being a vegetarian, the only steak I ever enjoy is the one they use to kill vampires on *Buffy*; and the only time I've been comfortable around a barbie was when I used my sister's dolls to act out scenes from *Casablanca*. (I wish that wasn't a true story.)

But here is the pizza de résistance: I once got a flat tyre on my Barina – yes, hello ladies – and when the NRMA couldn't come for an hour, I rang my mum, who talked me through changing it.

I rest my case. Yes, ladies and gentlemen, in a National Blokes Ranking I think I would be slightly in front of Kevin Rudd, but waaay behind Amanda Vanstone.

As if I needed further confirmation that I am a compromised male, a visit from the local plumbers put the final nail in the coffin (and no, I didn't hammer it).

As someone who chose comedy as a job because it's indoors with no heavy lifting, I greatly admire people who actually work for a living. Plus, with plumbers I feel we're kind of in the same line of work: it's just that I talk it and they make sure it gets flushed away.

Anyway, at the end of a long day with them working in the sun and me awkwardly lingering, I decided to try and bond with the bonza blokes by getting them a bloody beer. (Sorry, I learned everything I know about bloke-talk from Alf Stewart on *Home and Away*.)

So I went to the fridge looking for a good bloke's beer like VB or Tooheys, only to be greeted by a range of designer ales with titles so complex they sounded like they were named after Bob Geldof's kids. You know, the sort of beers that are from so far away they had to spend a month in Nauru before they were allowed in the country. I like to think of them as health foods, because they're all served with a slice of fruit in the neck.

Think of it this way: if VB comes with a David Boon doll, then the beers in my fridge should come with action figures of the cast of *Queer Eye for the Straight Guy*. Instead of asking for beer and nachos, they'd say, 'Those shoes don't go with those pants!' (While we're on the topic, if VB comes with a Boonie doll, does a bottle of red wine come with a Stuart MacGill doll? And if you stop on the way home for a packet of smokes and some condoms, do you get a novelty Warnie doll? You might want to keep that one separate from your other toys though, he might try to shag your Strawberry Shortcake.)

I was so embarrassed by my poncey ales I ended up pouring the beer into glasses for the plumbers and writing 'VB' on the outside in texta. As you can imagine, this experience didn't do much for my sense of self as a red-blooded Australian male, so shortly afterwards I made a resolution: I was going to try and become more of a man.

Now, I should quickly point out that I didn't mean this in the Matt Shirvington sense. I wasn't about to shove some socks down my jocks or enlist some backyard plastic surgeon to 'pimp my ride'. No, I decided it was time to pull on some overalls, get my hands dirty and hide in the shed, just like all the real Aussie blokes out there. As a consequence, I've been doing so much nailing and screwing of late that my friends have nicknamed me 'Lara Bingle'.

Yes, that's right, in the last few months I've spent nearly every waking moment doing odd jobs – which doesn't mean I've been having an affair with a James Bond villain, although due to a painting mishap I do now have a gold finger. (By the way, I have no idea why tasks such as putting up shelves are called 'odd jobs'. Milking a rat for a living, now that would be an odd job.)

I'm obsessed. You've heard of born-again Christians? Well, I'm a born-again tradesman. I have seen the light, and then installed it myself.

Not that my home renos are any good, I should point out. You'd see less streaks at a nudist colony than on my paint job; my shelves are like the ABC board – they lean heavily to the right; and even an asthmatic wolf who'd just walked up a flight of stairs could probably blow my house down.

And while my girlfriend is very happy that things are getting fixed around the house, she's not so happy about the amount of crack I've started to show out the back of my daks. Plus, she says the full-size poster of Scott Cam above the bed has to go.

But I digress. If being a home handyman is my new religion, then my church is Bunnings and I'm praying five times a day. I love Bunnings, and lately I've been there so often the staff must be starting to think I'm a stalker. Although I must confess, the real reason I have to go there numerous times a day is that I don't know what I'm doing so I keep forgetting to buy stuff: 'Oh, so you're saying I need brushes to put the paint on the wall?'

Luckily the staff are so damn helpful. It's like *DIY for Dummies*. They're so full of answers that if I ever went on *Who Wants to Be a Millionaire* I would use the local Bunnings as my call-a-friend. Although they do seem to be sick of me picking up a screwdriver and saying, 'This is not a drill', then grabbing a bag of nails and singing, 'Stop . . . hammer time!'

Not that they complain. Mr Bunnings has just put a new wing on his house due to my financial contribution. In two months I went from a bloke whose only experience with screwdrivers was drinking them, to someone who has more tools than an audition for *Australian Idol*. I now have so many hammers, nails, saws, hooks, files and screws that I had to go back to the hardware store to buy more wood to build a box to store them all. I'm even thinking of putting hooks on the wall and painting outlines for my various tools – you know, the ones that make it look like your tools have been murdered and are about to be investigated by *Law & Order: Special Hardware Unit*.

I've bought so much crap I will never need. I got an electric sander so powerful they say Camilla Parker Bowles uses the same one to take off her make-up. The other day I almost bought a ride-on lawnmower, even though we don't actually have a lawn. That's like Paris Hilton buying a book of brain-teasers.

But hands down, my favourite gadget is my electric drill. I went crazy with my new toy. My house now has more holes in it than the plot of *The Da Vinci Code*. Seriously folks, if I painted the walls in my place yellow you'd think they were made from Swiss cheese.

Yes, I think it's time to make a confession. 'Hi, I'm Wil and I'm a Bunnings-aholic.' I'm so bad, when I was at karaoke the other night I asked the deejay to play the Bunnings theme. When I saw the ad for more staff at my local shop I seriously considered applying just so I'd get the staff discount.

And is it wrong for me to think about proposing to my girlfriend just so we can have the bridal registry at Bunnings?

Come on ladies, surely nothing says love like an orbital sander?

I guess I've got weddings on my mind because my brother recently asked me to be his best man. Now, obviously, this is exciting, partly because I love him and I'm honoured to be a part of such an important day in his life, but mostly I'm excited because I love the title 'best man'.

You see, in my 35 years of life I haven't often been referred to as the 'best' at anything. And to be honest, given my personal history earlier, I'm just happy to be officially referred to as a 'man'.

The last time I was asked to be best man was for my friend Shep, but that time I was one of three. Yep, that's right, three. Now, while three is a fine number for musketeers, amigos, tenors, witches and blind mice, to me it seems a little excessive for best men.

Not wanting to seem ungrateful, I quietly asked Shep why he felt the need to enlist three separate best men. He gave me a look (which at the time I thought was of respect and concern, but I now recognise as pity) and simply said, 'Well, mate, you all have your individual strengths.'

I should have let it go, but I just had to ask. 'So, what are the other best men's individual strengths?' Without hesitation, he replied, 'Well, they're very trustworthy and reliable. I'm looking to them to organise the bucks' party, help me choose the ring, hire the suits, arrange the cars and make sure the bar is well-stocked all night at the reception.'

By now the voice inside my head was screaming, *Don't ask, run away now, keep the little remaining self-respect you're desperately clinging onto . . . whatever you do, just don't ask!* But I had to ask. I looked him directly in the eye and said, 'So what are my individual strengths, then?'

He paused, which I knew wasn't a great sign, and slowly replied, 'Well, um, I was hoping you might, er, make a funny speech and then get off with one of the bridesmaids!' And I'm proud to say, ladies and gentlemen, that on that wedding night I was two from two. (Well, OK, the speech wasn't that funny.)

So, although I'm always happy to oblige, in my view the title 'best man' is a little overstated. For starters, your presence is certainly less important than, say, the groom's, which immediately relegates you to 'second-best man'. Then, of course, in most cases the priest is also male (and if you believe in that sort of thing, has a direct line to God), so that knocks you down the order again. And that's without even considering that more often than not the father of the bride is present, which means that you don't even get to stand on the podium, but come in as the 'fourth-best man'.

Don't even get me started on gay weddings where there are two grooms, two fathers of the bride, and I guess probably two best men, as well.

In fact, now that I think about it, the only way the title 'best man' could be appropriate is if two lesbians, each of whom had been raised by two lesbians, were getting married and had a female celebrant.

But I digress.

I'm excited, but also nervous. I have only one brother, and even if I'm really the fourth-best man, I still want to make sure I do a good job. Thanks to Shep, I have experience in the speech bit, so that's covered, but as for the rest – I have no idea. Do I get a stripper? (For the bucks' party, obviously; even I know it would be in bad taste at the church.) The problem is, I've never been a massive fan of strip clubs. To me it's like taking a starving man to a restaurant, letting him look at the food and smell the food, but then making him go home hungry.

But I don't want to be the boring bucks' bloke. I decided I needed some help, so I called a recently married mate and asked him to tell me my responsibilities as best man.

'Don't worry mate, it's a piece of piss,' he said. 'You just get a nice black suit, a cool car, say a few profound words and fight crime.' At this point I realised that due to the bad reception in my house he'd thought I'd asked him what my responsibilities were as Batman.

I decided to go to the internet instead. After spending a few minutes looking at sites that seemed to skip the wedding and concentrate instead on the wedding night, I finally found what I was looking for: The Comprehensive Guide to Being a Best Man.

'Step One,' I read, 'above all else, be organised and offer constant moral support.'

My shoulders slumped in despair. Organisation and moral support are my two Achilles heels. (I know you're only meant to have one Achilles heel, but bugger it, we have two heels so I think it's only fair.)

Above all else, I am really badly organised. For a moment I actually thought, 'Would it be inappropriate to get my manager to organise my brother's bucks' party?' And when it comes to moral support, well, let's just say I don't have a foolproof barometer when it comes to knowing where to draw the line. The devil on my shoulder whispers in my ear, I wait for the angel to say something, and then realise the devil spiked his drink.

I guess the best I can do is keep reassuring my bro that he is doing the right thing, and if he changes his mind at the last moment, to make sure he has a car full of petrol and a glove box full of plane tickets, false passports and Tony Mokbel's old wigs.

I read on. 'Step Two: Organise measurements for suits, and pick up the groom's outfit on the day.'

What? Organise measurements? Am I really meant to do that? What is this, *Queer Eye for the Engaged Guy*? And what if his measurements change before the big day? Am I meant to keep ringing him to say, 'So dude, you still making it to the gym? I'm sending you a couple of vouchers for Bikram yoga!'

As it turns out, my bro is picking up his own suit, which is probably a good idea, as I'm likely to leave it to the last moment and then just take whatever is left ... and it would be embarrassing to hear the priest say, 'Do you,

Kelly, take ... um, er ... well it seems to be SpongeBob SquarePants ...'

Luckily, the next few steps seemed a little easier.

I was happy to dance with the bridesmaids (as long as they knew the 'Macarena', 'YMCA', 'Time Warp' or 'Nutbush'); I was prepared to organise the tossing of the garter (although if there weren't enough single men, I wondered if I could invite those whose relationships were a bit rocky); and I was even happy to sign the marriage licence. (I'll just have to be careful not to go with my usual: 'Thanks for watching, all the best, Wil.')

But my palms started to sweat as we came to the Big One. 'Final Step: Look after the ring!' Your main job, above all else, is to take care of and guard with your life the ring, until the vital moment when it can be taken out of your palm and flung into the fires of Mordor. (Oh, sorry, I got distracted for a minute by *Lord of the Rings* on Foxtel.)

The other day my brother confided that he's really nervous about the wedding, which I can certainly understand. From the bloke's point of view, there are just so many things that can go wrong on your wedding day.

First there are the all-important vows. Now, some blokes do write their own, but I advised my brother that if he chose to do this, he should make sure the vows were original and from the heart. One groom at a wedding I went to in the country simply reworked the words to the VB ad. It's fair to say that his missus wasn't impressed when he said, 'I love you milking a cow, or pulling a plough, matter of fact, I love you now!'

I advised my bro to go for the KISS approach, and by that I didn't mean put on make-up and sing, 'I Was Made for Lovin' You' with a cucumber shoved down the front of his leather pants. I meant KISS as in 'Keep It Simple, Stupid'.

As a bloke, I told him, all you really need to get right on the day are two words: 'I do.' (Well, that, and making sure you say them after the priest asks, 'Do you?' and not after he says, 'Does anyone have any objections?')

Some other important things I advised him to remember:

When his new wife throws the bouquet, he shouldn't think this is a great opportunity to fly over the back of the pack to take a 'speccy'.

Even though a wedding should have 'something old, something new, something borrowed, something blue', this is not an excuse to do some of his favourite Kevin Bloody Wilson material.

Most importantly, he must make sure he gets a priest who knows his lines.

I once went to a wedding where the clearly nervous young priest was trying to say, 'Sarah, you will know Darren's love by his ring on your finger.' A lovely sentiment, I think you'll all agree. Unfortunately, what he actually said was, 'Sarah, you'll know Darren's love by his finger on your ring.'

In my experience, I confess, that certainly *is* a way to learn that someone loves you – or is concerned about your prostate — but it's possibly not the Hallmark moment my brother would want his wedding day remembered for. (Possibly his honeymoon night, if that's his thing.)

Then we tackled the challenge of the bridal waltz. I advised my brother to choose a song that accurately summed up his relationship — unlike the couple at a wedding I once went to whose first dance together was to — and I swear this is true — U2's 'I Still Haven't Found What I'm Looking For'.

The thing about weddings is that they force you to confront your own relationship status. When my brother asked me to be best man, I'd been single for quite a while. Speaking candidly, I was desperate and dateless. So desperate that one night my eyes started lingering over the personal ads.

As far as I can tell from my brief survey, the most common requirement of single women is someone with 'a good sense of humour'. This sounds good, but I'm not sure it's entirely true. If this was what girls were really looking for, they'd be tearing down their posters of Owen Wilson and drooling over Kevin Bloody Wilson. (Furthermore, it should be pointed out that when women say they're looking for a man to make them laugh, it usually doesn't mean they want someone 'funny looking'.)

Another massive cliché of personal ads is, 'I enjoy long walks on the beach.' If it's a guy, that usually means, 'While I'm using my mobile phone to take photos of topless women'; and if it's a girl, it means, 'I like sitting on the couch in my tracksuit pants with a hot-water bottle and a block of chocolate watching *Beaches*.'

My brief study of personal ads has already taught me a few lessons – such as, when someone says, 'I've never done this before' it usually means, 'I've done this before, but I don't want you to think that I'm a desperate loser.'

When someone says they 'like the simple things in life', this generally means, 'I am poor.' (Coincidentally, 'I like the simple things in life' was apparently the pick-up line Laura Bush used to snag George.) And when someone says they're 'petite', it usually means they're short. When someone says they're 'curvy', it means they're fat. And when someone claims to 'like working with their hands', it means they didn't go to uni. I have to admit, though, 'petite, curvy and like working with my hands' sounds a lot more enticing than 'short, fat and dumb'.

If you study the personals closely you'll also find there are some warning signs to look out for. Like when someone feels the need to point out: 'I'm normal', it's code for 'I'm not normal . . . in fact, I have seventy-two cats and there's a real chance that I'll end up making a coat of your skin!'

When someone stresses 'I'm normal', it means they're actually a little bit crazy; but interestingly, when someone feels the need to point out they're 'a little bit crazy' it doesn't mean they're normal. It probably means they are 'a little bit crazy'.

Oh, and when someone says they're looking for a soul mate, that's code for, 'I'm really full-on, and if you dump me I will most likely stalk you.' (Let's be realistic here, folks, if you're looking for your soul mate in the personal ads, you're probably aiming a little high. Maybe settle for a mate who likes soul music, or even just one who isn't an R-soul.)

'Easy-going' is a little more difficult to decode. Does that mean they won't mind if you leave your coffee cup in the sink or put your feet on the couch? Or does it mean they wear the same underwear seven days in a row?

When someone describes themselves as 'adventurous', what exactly does that mean? Does it imply that their copy of the *Kama Sutra* has a few pages of their own notes stapled at the back? Does it mean they're willing to take a punt on the Ethiopian restaurant at the end of the street, or that their idea of a great date is a handful of nuts at the base station of Mount Everest?

'Athletic' is another interesting one. Does it mean they can walk up an escalator without needing an oxygen tent, that they go for the occasional jog or that they will require a urine sample at the end of the date?

When someone says they're searching for 'a partner in crime', this probably means they want someone to have some fun with. It probably doesn't mean that they'll lend you their stockings for an armed hold-up or help you bury a body.

It's also important to note that some things sound better on paper. For example, 'I'll try anything once' sounds really exciting – until you realise that Charles Manson would probably describe himself the same way. Let's face it, when you ask, during a romantic dinner with your partner,

'Wow, this is really tasty, what's the secret ingredient?' you don't want to hear, 'People ... now rub the lotion on your skin!'

And some descriptions are just downright confusing. Like when someone claims they're 'not into playing games', does that mean mind-games, or do they have some deep-seated aversion to Hungry Hungry Hippos?

Or when someone says they are looking for 'chemistry', does it mean a) someone they have a spark with? b) someone who passed chemistry in their HSC, or c) someone who knows how to make speed in their basement?

Finally, for a lot of people in singles ads it seems that smoking is a major turn-off. Personally, I like to date someone who smokes, because every conversation sounds like heavy breathing.

But the weirdest thing about the nonsmoking request is the type of ads in which it occurs. Someone will say, 'I'm looking for a partner who likes to dress head to toe in a leather priest outfit and take my confession while spanking me ... no smokers!' Yes, because you wouldn't want to attract anyone with antisocial habits.

I guess there are some benefits to being single. You don't have to worry about Valentine's Day, for one thing. And this is a particular relief to me, because when it comes to getting lucky on 14 February, I don't have a great track record. In fact, when I was at uni, a girl even broke up with me on Valentine's Day. Being aware of my love of Dr Seuss, she left me a card that said, 'I do not like green eggs and ham . . . or you!'

Being single on Valentine's Day really sucks. I think it's completely unfair that couples get a whole day dedicated to their love. After all, they already have someone to have sex with — surely that should be reward enough? But no, they have to go and rub it in with Valentine's Day, V-Day, the old VD. (OK, that was going a bit far.) A day that might as well be called, 'Nyah nyah nyah, Everybody Loves Me, Nobody Likes You Day'.

Seriously, why do people who already have love and companionship need a special day? What about the forgotten people? Where's 'I've Never Had a Girlfriend (Unless You Count Lara Croft) Day', 'The Only Love I Recognise Is That Between Frodo and Sam Day', or 'If You Want to Love Me You Have to Love My Seventy-two Cats Day'?

But no, instead it's the people who've already found their soul mate who get the dinner, flowers, chocolates and delightful helium balloons on a stick. It just doesn't seem fair. Surely the people in love should have to give the single losers a delightful helium balloon on a stick? Better still, how about a special day where everyone in a happy relationship has to give a sympathy shag to someone who's single. We could call it Warnie Day.

(What is Valentine's Day, anyway? If Christmas is when Jesus was born and Easter is when he died, is Valentine's Day when he went on a date with Mary Magdalene? Oh yeah, I read *The Da Vinci Code*.)

But without doubt, my major problem with the big 14 February has to be the soppy greeting cards with sentiments so sweet you risk developing diabetes just reading them. Does anyone actually swallow this crap? One year I'd like to see Hallmark bring out a range of brutally honest greeting cards, such as, 'Roses are red, violets are blue, if this gets any more sickly, I think I will spew', or 'Roses are red, and I think that you're cute, but if you really like flowers, then how about a root?'

Why stop there? Sometimes the biggest challenge in a relationship is being completely honest with your partner – so how much easier would it be if you could simply pick up a $3 card inscribed with the exact sentiment you're after? Like, 'Here's some choccies and flowers – in fact, I bought you a wreath – but please, a little less tongue, it's like you're cleaning my teeth'; 'The dinner was yummy, the chocolates delicious, but this Valentine's Day I'd prefer you did the dishes'. Or if you really want to get to the point, 'It's a day for chocolates and roses, and they'll get you far, but if you really want some action, then buy me a car.'

This new range of cards would also come in very handy for people in relationships who get presents they don't really want: 'I love you, my darling, but you are a loony, if you think you'll drink all the beer and just give me Boonie'. Or for the blokes: 'Roses are red, violets are blue, you bought me a hammer, when all I wanted was a screw.'

Those in relationships often use Valentine's Day to make up

for some of the mistakes they've made during the year. But yet again, it's hard to find the card that expresses the exact sentiment you're after. 'I bought you some chocolates, if you like them I'm glad, and I'm really sorry I said you kissed like your dad!'; or 'You're smart, funny and cute, I hope our love never ends, just like I hope you don't find out that I shagged your best friend!'

Of course, not everyone is caught up in the spirit of romance, but those people are another potential market: 'It's Valentine's Day, but we both think it's stupid, so I bought you a gun, let's go hunting for Cupid'; or 'Your new boy bought you flowers, they were red and smelly, but while you were at dinner, I stole your telly!'

How about a range of cards for those whose relationships have ended badly? 'Flowers are great, but every rose has a thorn, now I've got a new boyfriend, and you're home watching porn'; 'Here's a bunch of balloons, I bought them with cash, I hope they're a surprise like when you gave me that rash'; 'Roses are red, that's not debatable, but you shouldn't buy roses – your new girlfriend's inflatable'; or even 'I got you balloons because I think that you blow, and this isn't a card, it's a rhyming AVO!'

If you want to be really creative, how about a range of e-cards for romances that started on the internet? 'Roses are red, so are your cheeks, sucker, you thought you'd emailed a hottie, but I'm really a trucker'; or 'You're as hot as Windows 2005, so let me turn your floppy disk into a hard drive.'

And finally, who wouldn't find this card handy: 'I know you were hoping for romance this Valentine's Day, but I've got something to tell you: I'm secretly gay!'

All bitterness and guile aside, once you're in a relationship, Valentine's Day can actually be quite useful. You see, when it comes to commemorating Cupid's favourite day, blokes seem to fall into three distinct categories. First, there are the cynics who think it's all a moneymaking conspiracy perpetrated by the teddy bear barons and novelty-balloon-making mafia. Then there are the hopeless romantics, who seem to spend 364 days of every year trying to come up with words that rhyme with 'love', 'Cupid' and 'shnookums'.

And finally, there is my favourite group: the blokes who treat the romance of Valentine's Day a lot like a visit to the dentist — you put up with it for one day so you don't have to worry about it again for the rest of the year.

It's this final mob that got me thinking. If you're going to use Valentine's Day to get your romance out of the way for twelve months, why stop there? Why not come up with a series of theme days on which blokes could knock over other things they pretend to like in relationships so they don't have to worry about them again for another 365 days?

Think about it. You could have 'Notice that You Have a New Dress/Haircut/Shoes Day', 'I'll Tell You I Love You Even When My Mates Are Listening Day', or even 'Hey, You Know What We Should Do on the Weekend? Go Shopping Day'.

Or what about 'It's OK, You Can Be in Charge of the Remote Day', where, in a very romantic gesture, you hand over your most valued possession and let your lovely lady choose what you watch for an entire night. Forget flowers, when it comes to your average bloke, there's nothing that says 'I love you' more than relinquishing control over the remote. Especially if it's accompanied by a card that says, 'Darling, I love you, so tonight let's get steamy, switch on *Grey's Anatomy* and we'll drool over McDreamy!'

This would, of course, be followed by 'Watching Movies That You Choose Day' (aka 'Go Sick, Pick a Chick Flick Day'), a 24-hour period dominated by *Dirty Dancing*, *Beaches*, the entire back catalogue of John Hughes, and enough Hugh Grant to last a lifetime. Sure, there'd be so much sugar you'd run the risk of getting toothache, but imagine the rewards as she turns to you afterwards and whispers, 'Thank you, my love, I know you think these movies stink, but from now on it's *The Rock* and *Transformers*, not *Pretty in Pink*!'

And who wouldn't mind getting all those awkward conversations out of the way on 'Look, We Really Need to Talk Day'. Everything from 'So where do you see this relationship heading?' to 'So, what do you think of kids?' and, of course, 'Look, if you don't ask me to marry you soon I'm going to start sleeping with your friends!' (For those who want to save time, 'Look, We Really Need to Talk Day' could be easily combined with 'Why Don't We Just Talk About Our Feelings Day'.)

While we're on the topic of awkward conversations, we might as well declare 'There is No Way I Can Answer That Question Without Getting in Trouble Day'. Think about it blokes, wouldn't it be great to know that for the rest of the year there'd be no risk of being asked, 'What are you thinking right now?', 'Do you ever fantasise about other girls when you're with me?' or 'Would you still love me if I had no arms?'

I'd almost look forward to opening my card in the morning and reading, 'I love to ask you hard questions, and today is my chance, but from now on I won't ask "Do I look fat in these pants?"'

This could be followed by 'Pretending I Don't Find Your Friends Hot Day'. This one is quite self-explanatory, but maybe to save time it could be run in conjunction with 'What Hot Girl? I Didn't Even Notice Day', 'Of Course I Don't Check Out Topless Women at the Beach Day' and 'Of Course I Never Look at Porn on the Internet Day'.

And while I'm not one myself, I certainly know a few blokes who would be happy to celebrate 'Give Your Partner a Foot Massage Day' if it meant they could get it out of the way for the rest of the year.

I don't mind giving the foot rub, but mates of mine have confessed that they hate it so much they intentionally do it badly in the hope that their partners won't ask them again. (They probably don't use the same excuse for their love-making.) Imagine the Hallmark card for that situation: a calloused foot on the front, and inside the poem, 'Today my dear, I'll give your toes a rub, but for the rest of the year, I'll be at the pub.'

If these catch on, we could add some others. What about 'Going to the Markets (And Not Complaining) Day', 'It's OK Honey, You Drink and I'll Drive Tonight Day', 'I Know We're Lost So I Will Pull Over and Ask For Directions Day', 'Sure You Can Pick the Pimples on My Back Day', 'Of Course I Would Like to Spend the Day With Your Ex Day', 'I'll Get the Hot-water Bottle and Rub Your Tummy Day', 'I'll Take My Socks Off in Bed Day' and, of course, 'We Don't Need to Have Sex, Why Don't We Just Hold Each Other? Day'.

❋ ❋ ❋

Have you ever buggered up a handshake? I did the other day: I went to shake the hand of a bloke I'd just met, misjudged, and got just fingers. Before I knew it, his hand had been pulled away and it was over.

It completely threw me. I spent the next five minutes not even listening, just haunted by the fact that I'd given this bloke such a shocking shake and wishing I could ask for a do-over. You see, I pride myself on having pretty good handshake skills. When I was growing up, my dad always said to me, 'Stop it or you'll go blind' but also, 'You can tell a lot about a person by the way they shake hands.'

According to Dad, the first rule of shaking someone's hand is you should look them in the eye – unless, of course, they're cross-eyed, in which case try to aim for their forehead. And if they're completely blind, use your other hand to go through their wallet. (Dad also told me if you are shaking hooks with a pirate, look them directly in the patch.)

Now, when it comes to firmness, I like to use the Goldilocks rule: not too hard, not too soft; or if you prefer the breakfast cereal analogy, not too heavy, not too light, just right. There's nothing worse than someone who goes too hard and instead of shaking your hand, tries to juice it. Well, actually, there is one thing worse: the person whose shake is so soft you feel like giving their hand a squirt of the Ugly Dave Grey nasal spray.

I hate the wet-fish handshake. If someone's previously given me the wet fish, next time I just refuse to shake their hand. I'm like John West: it's the wet fish I reject that make my handshakes the best.

Here's another for young players: when it comes to handshakes, if we don't know each other, let's keep it simple. Let's not try one of those complicated gangsta handshakes unless we have a choreographer and some rehearsals. Sometimes people shake your hands in such a way that you think you've a) just joined a secret organisation, b) have to steal third, or c) have to meet a guy on a bridge at midnight with a suitcase full of cash.

Oh, and here's another tip. Once we've shaken hands, it's time to let go. There's nothing worse than someone who continues to hold your hand for the duration of the conversation. What's next, dude? Are we going to start skipping down the street?

And while some people favour the double-hand shake, I think it should be avoided unless you're the Pope, a politician on the campaign trail or congratulating an old lady on her prize-winning scones.

Another question I often get asked is, 'How many times should you pump it?' To which I say, 'Didn't you hear what my dad said? Stop it or you'll go blind!'

However, when it comes to handshakes, I usually aim for more than one pump, but no more than three. Some people pump your arm like they think you're a poker machine, and if they pull enough times gold coins will start shooting out your bum.

Oh, here's another tip. When you're shaking my hand, don't also touch my elbow. I know it's meant to indicate intimacy, but if I'd wanted you to touch my elbow I would have offered it to you in the first place.

Another thing that freaks me out is people who shake your hand and then drape their other arm around your shoulder. For me, this one is only appropriate if you're giving me some sort of award and we're posing for a photo.

Then there's the delicate issue of women. When it comes to women and handshakes, things can be a little confusing these days. Some like the kiss, some the shake; all I'm certain of is if a girl offers you her hand, shake it, don't kiss it, unless you've stepped into a time-machine and travelled back fifty years.

Of course, just when you thought that handshakes were complicated enough, these days you have to throw hugs into the mix, too. When is it appropriate for a bloke to hug another bloke as a greeting? Clearly it's fine if you've just scored a try, or taken some ecstasy (or both, in the case of Andrew Johns). But what about the rest of the time?

These days it seems totally fine to hug another man in public – although if you want to give them a cuddle or do some spooning, I suggest you at least buy them a drink first.

As far as I can tell, most men seem to like the hug where you hug and simultaneously pat the other person on the back. It's kind of like saying, 'Look, I know I'm hugging you, but don't get the wrong idea. I'm also hitting you at the same time!'

I have to confess, I'm actually a fan of the hug, although there are some people I still wouldn't hug – such as my boss, my bank manager and my PE teacher.

But in the end, the most important thing is to decide whether to hug or shake. You've got to choose one or the other. What you *don't* want is to end up in a situation where one of you goes for the handshake and the other goes for the hug and the hand ends up getting jammed between you in such a way that you are not only hugging, but also technically engaged to be married.

Ah, social awkwardness. While we're on the topic, a question: is there anything worse than coming up with the perfect comeback for an insult about thirty seconds after the moment has passed?

OK, clearly there are a heap of worse things, like having to listen to an iPod that only contains Daryl Somers' solo albums or being forced to drink all the sweat shed by contestants on *The Biggest Loser* – and that's just to name a couple off the top of my head. But I do think it's fair to say that the only thing worse than being insulted by someone is coming up with the perfect witty rejoinder when the conversation has already moved on. You almost feel like saying, 'Wait . . . you know that thing you said before about my shirt . . . when you said a caravan somewhere was missing its curtains, that it looked like something even Dr Karl would reject for being too loud? Yeah, say that again, I'm ready now.'

Sometimes I feel like my entire life is just a succession of those moments. The latest one happened the other day as my girlfriend and I were walking through the make-up section of a major department store. Out of nowhere a security guard slammed into Amy, sending her flying so far I thought she was going to have to get permission from air-traffic control to land.

He seriously knocked her into a different postcode. Luckily, she was OK – well, apart from the $10 cab-ride she had to take to get back to where she started. The thing is, the whole episode could have been sorted out with a quick apology. Sadly, though, for this security guard sorry seemed to be the hardest word to say. (And probably to spell as well.)

Now, before I go on, I should point out that I'm not a believer in 'the customer is always right' thing, especially if the customer is trying to buy a copy of James Blunt's *Greatest Hits*. But in this case, the customer was not only right, but courtesy of Clumsy-Security-Guard Air had clocked up enough frequent flyer miles to get a free trip to Perth and back.

But still no apology – in fact, it was getting to the stage where our former prime minister was more likely to pop in and say 'sorry' than this dude was.

So my beautiful bruised babe decided the best course of action was to let fly with a string of expletives. If she'd been on *Big Brother* it would have sounded like a truck backing up. (It's fair to say she included some turns of phrase that would have made Kevin Bloody Wilson and Adam Selwood from the West Coast Eagles blush.)

At this point, our security guard could have simply said 'touché' and called it a draw; but no. He started insulting her, her family and her upbringing.

This was when I decided to step in. Not because Amy can't take care of herself, but because I didn't want to spend all afternoon helping her hide a body in the bush.

I began by trying to talk to the security guard very calmly. It soon became clear that he was the kind of bloke who put on his black T-shirt in the morning, forgot he was guarding free Clinique sample bags and mistook himself for Clint Eastwood in *In the Line of Fire*. You know how some people go on power trips? Well, this boofhead had booked a power-round-the-world vacation.

So I decided the best course of action would be to get his name and make a complaint later. Unfortunately, when I asked for it he refused, saying he couldn't tell me (even though 'Barry' was clearly printed on his badge) and then started insulting me. 'What, you're a lawyer now, are you?!' he scoffed.

Now, I should point out that I'm not the sort of person who judges someone's intelligence based on their job, but since he started it . . .

'Hmmm, interesting point mate, but I'm thinking that if one of us should be pondering our level of education it's the bloke whose job it is to make sure teenage Goths don't steal too much foundation!'

Actually, I didn't say any of that. I thought of it about thirty seconds too late. But it was quickly becoming clear to me that the number seventy on this bloke's shirt wasn't just his ID, it was his IQ. Working security at a nightclub would have been too complex for this dude. If someone told him their name was on the door, he'd think they were called Mr No-Shoes-No-Shirt-No-Service.

Even though he was being a dick, I did feel a bit sorry for him. After all, I'm guessing that at the local security guards' union meeting, the coolest blokes are those who guard rock stars, presidents and suitcases full of cash, not lipstick and cherry-flavoured gloss. The make-up floor is hardly what you'd consider action-packed — although some nannas can get pretty vicious at the Boxing Day sales. The only time our bloke would come home with a black eye is if he had too much mascara put on during a demo. And how often would someone radio the order, 'Someone's used too many of the free samples . . . shoot to kill'?

But my sympathy quickly drained when he looked at me smugly and said, 'Well, you don't know my last name, how are you going to identify me?'

I thought for a moment and came up with the perfect comeback: 'Well, I'll just tell them it was Barry, the fat security guard from the make-up section with the stupid goatee and glasses. I'll think they'll be able to work it out!' The only downside was by the time I said this Barry had already walked away and left me talking to myself in the middle of the make-up department.

SEVEN

SURVIVAL OF THE FATTEST

They say the terror suspects arrested at Heathrow airport a few years ago were caught with substances that couldn't be identified by British authorities. When I returned from the UK after a month at the Edinburgh Fringe Festival, I knew what they were talking about: those 'substances' were probably fresh fruit and vegetables.

I know it's a cliché, but I reckon the food in Scotland is so unhealthy that you can actually feel your arteries harden as you eat. After all, this is the country that invented deep-fried pizza. (Oh, and the Mars Bar. Yes, a deep-fried Mars Bar a day helps you work, rest, play and die of a massive coronary.)

There's a very good reason you don't see many elderly Scottish people. I was only there a month, but I packed on five kilograms. My body shape changed completely. My gut became really big from all the deep-fried food and late-night drinking, but my legs got really skinny from walking up the hills. I was beginning to think that maybe ET wasn't from outer space – he was from Edinburgh.

Not only is everything covered in batter, it's also covered in brown sauce. Have you heard of this stuff? I mean, if tomato sauce is made of tomatoes, and apple sauce is made of apples, what the hell is brown sauce made of? It's a case for *CSI: Edinburgh*.

I'm sorry, but when I think 'brown', my immediate thoughts are 'dirt', 'Bobby' and 'poo'; and I wouldn't want to spread any of them on my chips. (Although on the upside, they will come out the same colour as they went in.) Put it this way, you know the chow isn't wow when you actually look forward to the flight home so you can eat some decent airline food.

On the way back to Oz, I had spinach pasta on the plane that probably came out of a can and went straight into a microwave, but it tasted like Neil Perry had prepared it on Scarlett Johansson's thighs.

I do have some standards when it comes to food, though I'm hardly what you'd call a gourmand. (And even if you did, I'd think you were saying I was fat.) It's not often that I get to go to really fancy restaurants. Having been a starving stand-up most of my life, my idea of fine dining is when the all-you-can-eat buffet comes with a plastic sneeze-guard.

SURVIVAL OF THE FATTEST

Most of the time I tend to chow down in dives where they don't have chef's hats on the door, they have cockroaches on the floor – and little flags on the tables, so the waiters remember where to deliver the grub. I must admit I'm quite fond of the flag: it makes me feel like I'm dining at an embassy or on the surface of the moon. 'It's one small bite for man, one giant bite for mankind.' Sometimes I'll even grab the flag, stick it in some food I like the look of on someone else's plate and claim it as my own.

That said, I do always splash out on a fancy restaurant for a date. I learned very early on that showing a girl you're a big spender by letting her upsize her fries is not going to lead to a McPash. She'll probably decide the boys are better at Hungry Jack's.

So, with this in mind, my girlfriend and I headed out for some posh nosh the other night. And the place we went to was fancy. Very fancy. Fancy as. Could not have been fancier if. It was one of those restaurants where they have a separate waiter for everything. They had a drinks waiter for the drinks, a food waiter for the food, a wine waiter for the wine – and they were all wearing better suits than most of my mates wore to their own weddings. I really didn't want to ask what the head waiter did.

And they all had such attitude! Put it this way, the bread may have been complimentary, but the staff were not. Our food waiter must have been very concerned about prostate cancer, because he had his head right up his bum.

It was also one of those places where the waiter puts the napkin on your lap. Now, this might not seem like a big deal to most folks, but I have to admit I really don't like it – well, unless the waitress is really hot, in which case I suddenly become extremely clumsy and drop my napkin . . . a lot.

But most of the time it just makes me feel like a baby – and not in the Madonna way. I half-expect them to follow up by putting a bib around my neck and mashing up my peas so they can play 'Here comes the choo choo train'. And if anything gets on my face, they'll spit on a hanky and wipe it off.

It was one of those restaurants where there seems to be too much cutlery on the table, too. There were more forks than there are in a Kevin Rudd speech, more knives than there are in Kim Beazley's back and more spoons than you would find on the floor of Pete Doherty's flat. (Yeah, I read the *Financial Review* and *New Weekly*.)

Before I go any further, I should point out that the food was fabulous, although I was initially a little suspicious about the rose petals in the entrée. That's right, rose petals. Obviously I have been taking Amy to the wrong places; instead of five-star restaurants I should have been taking her to the local florist for all-you-can-eat. If a strange man comes up to you in the street and gives you flowers, it may not be Impulse, it might just be takeaway.

But flowers in the fang aside, I knew for sure that it was truly a fancy-pants place to fill your food-hole when I saw

SURVIVAL OF THE FATTEST

the size of the meals. They were tiny. You know, the ones that are so small you think they've mistakenly only put some garnish on your plate, then you realise that's the meal.

'Um, excuse me, what happened to the rest of our food? Did the waiter get hungry on the trip from the kitchen to our table? Who is the chef here, Nicole Richie?'

Seriously folks, it got to the point where I was hoping they would spit in my food, because then it might actually fill me up. I guess at least it became clear why all the waiting staff were in black-tie – it was in case someone died of starvation and they had to attend the funeral.

To add insult to injury, they not only gave me an amount of food that I would normally refer to as 'leftovers', but they served it on a plate so big I started to suspect a sporting stadium was missing its roof. I know it's not a new phenomenon, but what is the idea behind the big plate? Is it meant to fool us into thinking we've eaten that much already? It just makes me more aware of how small the meal is. It's like buying a thirteen-year-old boy a packet of extra-large condoms.

Then they have the nerve to ask you if you'd like to order any sides. 'Well, actually mate, I'd like to order a pizza, but I guess some sides will have to do. Don't bother putting them in a bowl, you can just serve them on the side of my plate, there's plenty of room there.'

Anyway, needless to say I only left a small tip, although I did put it in the middle of a really big plate, so I don't think they'll notice.

While we're talking about food etiquette, when did ordering coffee become so complicated? There's something seriously wrong with the world when it takes you less time to drink the coffee than it does to order the bloody thing. At some of the newer chains you actually need a coffee just to have the energy to order one.

I should confess now that when it comes to coffee I'm hardly a connoisseur. In fact, I'd say I'm pretty old-school. I would like it to a) help me stay awake, b) not taste too much like dirt and c) be served in some sort of portable cup. And in the interests of full disclosure, I should also point out that if I'm going to have milk in my coffee, I'll order soy, not because I prefer the taste, but because – to the eternal disappointment of my dairy-farmer parents – I am lactose intolerant. It's kind of like Thorpie's kid being allergic to water, or Warnie's son being gay. (It turns out I'm actually intolerant of a lot of things: milk, onions and particularly people who check their account balance at the ATM before taking out money. I mean, you either have the money or you don't. Have a crack!)

But I digress. These days some people take drinking coffee very seriously. Some even think that the sort of coffee you drink reflects the kind of sexual partner you look for. Sadly, my girlfriend's favourite coffee – and I'm not making this up – is a weak, full-fat flat white.

People are definitely drinking more and more coffee, though. I am, anyway. You know you're drinking way too

SURVIVAL OF THE FATTEST

much when even the local ice addicts are looking at you like, 'Dude, you should slow down a little . . . I mean, have a nap or something!'

I have one mate who drinks so many lattes he got a podium placing in the Melbourne Formula 1 Grand Prix – and he wasn't even driving a car. He was just running around the track yelling, 'Vroom!'

Of course, you could order a decaf, but coffee without caffeine has always seemed a little like non-alcoholic beer to me – they both belong in the bin marked, 'What's the point?' Some people even order a decaf skim-milk coffee, which, as far as I can work out, is actually a glass of water.

But it gets worse. I know people who order their 'froth on the side'. What the . . . ? I mean, I kind of get it if you don't like froth, but what's the deal with having it on the side? Sure, someone on a diet might order salad dressing or butter on the side, but froth? I haven't read the articles closely, but I'm pretty sure the recent rise in childhood obesity isn't directly attributable to an excess of froth.

So, you can now order your coffee with milk on the side, sugar or honey on the side and froth on the side. Well, why stop there? Why not have the coffee on the side? And the water too! Why not just walk into Starbucks and order an empty cup with everything on the side? Or better still, just stay home and make a cup of coffee yourself.

(In case you think I'm being ridiculous here, the other day I heard someone order a 'no water coffee'. What does that mean? Do they just get you to open your mouth and shove a spoonful of Nescafé in your gob?)

As if all the new, complicated styles of coffee aren't enough, people also have all sorts of stupid slang words for their daily fix. I was having breakfast with a caffeine addict mate of mine the other day, and when I went to order he shouted out, 'Can you get me a Gary Coleman?' I studied the menu at the counter for about ten minutes before I realised he meant a short black.

And tell me this: when did everyone in the world become a barista? Maybe I'm wrong, but it was my understanding that in the old days this title used to imply that the person had a specific set of skills and expertise. Now it seems like any monkey they let fire up the cappuccino machine automatically qualifies. Surely that's like the pimply teen who cooks the fries at Maccas referring to himself as a chef, or the kid on the little aeroplane ride out the front of the local shopping centre calling himself a pilot?

Another thing: can anyone fill me in on when coffee cups became so big? There used to be two sizes: cup or mug. When did they decide to start serving it in buckets? Every time I walk out of a Starbucks I feel like I'm auditioning for the part of Jittery in a production of *Snow White and the Seven Dwarfs*.

I was in Tasmania the other day and ordered a small coffee. The cup I was presented with looked less like you could sip from it and more like Roger Federer should be raising it

SURVIVAL OF THE FATTEST

above his head after winning a tennis tournament. And that was the 'small'. The sizes went all the way up to extra-large! I mean, why the hell does anyone in Tassie need to drink that much coffee? I'll be perfectly honest with you, there really isn't that much stuff there that's worth staying awake for.

'Still,' you might point out, 'it's not coffee consumption that's giving Australia headaches, it's bingeing on booze, right?' Does Australia have a drinking problem? Well, I think there are three possible answers to this particular alcopop quiz.

1) Yes, and it's time to put politics to one side and have a sensible debate on how to ensure Australians drink safely and responsibly.
2) No, the only problem we have is when the booze runs out . . . now pass the lemon and salt.
3) What are you lookin' at? Yeah, you! Why don't you take a picture, it'll last longer. Excuse me, I think I need to be sick. Sorry about your shoes man, I love you, I really love you.

Now, I like a drink as much as the next bloke – as long as the next bloke is an Irish writer or Russian politician – but if we are to have a realistic and productive debate about Australia's drinking culture, first we have to acknowledge that Australia *has* a drinking culture.

And it does. After all, we live in a country where our two most famous sporting statistics are 99.94 and 52 – 99.94 is, of course, Sir Donald Bradman's batting average; 52 is the number of cans David Boon is rumoured to have consumed on a flight to London for an Ashes tour.

Most Aussies are not wowsers. A lot of us enjoy a drink. And I know it's not politically correct to say this in public anymore, but a lot of people enjoy a drink because — and let's linger on this for just a moment — drinking, when done responsibly, can be fun.

Bugger it, if we're being honest, let's be completely honest. Sometimes drinking is also fun when it is done irresponsibly. Some of my best memories are the ones I can't remember.

This is the dirty secret of the drinking debate. A lot of people drink to excess because it's fun. Yes, it can also be dangerous and destructive, but if we're going to move forward in this debate, we first have to acknowledge this simple but important point.

Regardless of what people might think is ideal in a perfect world, we live in a country in which a certain percentage of the population sees the recommended alcohol limit on booze packaging, not as a warning, but as a challenge.

These are people who, when they see the label 'Enjoy in Moderation', think Moderation must be some groovy new nightclub in the city.

And does this really surprise anyone? Remember this is a country where more people know the words to the VB ad than to the national anthem. We will never be able to fully combat the problems associated with binge drinking until we admit that a lot of ordinary Australians often drink to get drunk. After all, why go for a walk when you can run? And why go for a run when you can go to the pub?

So however hard the government might try to convince us, our problems are not going to be solved by raising taxes on RTDs, STDs or R2D2s if we don't first deal with the fact that, in our culture, if a news report suggests it's healthy to drink two glasses of wine a day, we tend to think, 'Well, imagine how healthy I'll feel if I drink two bottles a day! I'll be able to give up going to the gym!'

That's not to say we shouldn't be doing more to crack down on the clowns who can't drink properly, but I don't think the recent suggestion of putting cigarette-style warnings on the side of booze bottles will help. Does anyone want to see a bottle of wine plastered with a photo of a plastered Amy Winehouse?

We all know that cigarettes harm your unborn baby, but will it help to tell people that drinking beer will give them a gut that makes them look like they're having a baby?

And imagine diners in a fancy restaurant ordering a bottle of Grange Hermitage, to have the waiter respond, 'Would sir prefer the rotting liver or the rugby league player vomiting in the gutter?'

I mean, what would these warnings say?

'Warning: Consuming this may make those hot chicken rolls they sell in 7-Eleven seem more delicious than they really are.'

'Warning: May make you think it's a great idea to put an orange traffic cone on your head and pretend you're a witch on the way to a rave.'

'Warning: May make you think that it's a really good idea to call all your ex-girlfriends at four o'clock in the morning.'

'Warning: May result in you spending the night in Scores nightclub in New York and then getting elected Prime Minister of Australia.'

'Warning: Drinking may lead to smoking, and we all know how bad smoking is for you; haven't you read the warnings on the packets?'

However, I do agree with the suggestion that alcohol ads should be more realistic. Who wouldn't like to see a VB ad that went, 'You can get it getting kicked out of the cricket while wearing a watermelon on your head, you can get it not getting it up in bed, you can get it naked in a field in the middle of the night tipping over a cow ... matter of fact, I've got it now!'

One thing's for sure, waging a war on an addictive, habit-forming and mind-altering substance is never going to be easy. Anti-drug campaigns are mounted year after year, yet public health officials aren't coming any closer to victory.

You know the War on Drugs is over when even Michael Phelps is busted smoking a bong. I mean, the dude is possibly the greatest swimmer in the history of the Olympics; how can the powers-that-be use him as a bad example? 'Well, I know he might have won eight gold medals at the Olympic

SURVIVAL OF THE FATTEST

Games, but imagine how many more he would have won if he'd been motivated!'

In fact, the revelations that Phelps is a stoner make his achievements seem all the more remarkable. If I were the one smoking the pot, I wouldn't last half an hour without eating in order to actually get myself into the pool.

But it is true, dear readers, that Mr Phelps has done a major disservice to the kids ('Won't somebody please think of the children?'). Everyone knows that it's government policy to scare people off taking drugs by telling them that anyone who does so is a loser. It's hard to maintain this line in the wake of a bloke who has so much gold around his neck that he looks like Mr T smoking a bong. And all this time we just thought his eyes were red from the chlorine.

A bong.

And what a bong it was, too. It looked less like he was smoking marijuana and more like he was playing a weird glass didgeridoo. Apparently he got so stoned he tried to eat Stephanie Rice.

Sure, I knew he had great lung capacity in the pool, but this was taking things to a whole new level. During bushfires, instead of sending in helicopters filled with water, they should just send in Phelpsy with a length of garden hose.

And perhaps we shouldn't judge him too harshly. Maybe there's an innocent explanation for his aberrant behaviour. Maybe he's not very good at Latin and misunderstood the official Olympic motto, 'Faster, higher, swifter!' Or maybe pot is the reason for his motivation in the pool. Perhaps he wants to win so many medals because they're 'shiny!' (Although I imagine he was quite disappointed to find they didn't contain chocolate.)

At the end of the day, I don't really think it matters too much. I mean, pot is hardly a performance-enhancing drug, is it? Not that I'm completely against performance-enhancing drugs — well, theoretically, at least.

Think about it. The accepted wisdom seems to be that everyone — and I mean everyone — is anti-drugs in sport, right? But let's look at this logically. Shouldn't someone who knowingly takes a dangerous drug in order to win a gold medal for their country be labelled a hero?

Sure, most professional athletes are willing to get up early in the morning, train their guts out, watch what they eat and dedicate their mind to winning. But you have to ask the question: unless they're willing to fill themselves with untested illegal drugs, do they really care?

We always hear athletes say they want to give 110 percent. And how do they achieve that extra 10 percent? Drugs! Yes, to train hard and compete fairly takes heart; but to cheat well — that takes balls. Tiny, shrunken balls. And that's just the women.

Of course, when it comes to problematic substances, the alcopops and drugs debates pale in comparison to the frenzy that erupted over drinking recycled water.

I should first point out that I don't drink a lot of bottled water. I've never quite understood why someone would happily pay three bucks for something that comes out of the tap for free. I mean, if petrol came out of the kitchen tap, would people pop down to the servo to pay $3 for a 600 ml plastic bottle of unleaded just because it came from France?

That's why I also can't understand why people went so bananas about the price of bananas a few years ago. Yes, I know you shouldn't have to take out a second mortgage to make a smoothie (although it did mean that B1 and B2 were getting a lot more for their after-hours work), but here's a wacky idea folks: just don't eat bananas.

After all, they say the human body is 70 percent water, but nobody is 70 percent banana – well, with the possible exception of Matt Shirvington. (In fact, I've heard rumours he's renaming himself the Big Banana and opening his pants to tourists.)

My point is, if you renounce the yellow gold for a few months, is it really going to ruin your life? Sure, I like a banana split as much as the next slightly tubby fella, but if bananas were made illegal tomorrow I'm sure I'd cope. Actually, now that I think about it, with no annoying fruit to fill me up I could fit in delicious ice-cream, cream, topping and nuts. Or better still, just toss in some of those lolly bananas. Mmmm, lolly bananas.

But I digress. As I'm sure you've heard, the government recently mooted the idea of introducing recycled water for drinking purposes. Yep, while some people look at the glass as half-full and others as half-empty, the government is thinking about adding a third option: half flush.

And the proposition has certainly divided people. Some have pooh-poohed the plan, others are undeterred.

Before I continue with the barrage of puns, I should state for the record that I am a keen recycler. I recycle jokes all the time. In fact, I think I've even used that one before. (Oh yeah, I'm postmodern as!)

But – and this is a big but, think Serena Williams size – the truth is that when it comes to doo-doo, most people still really don't-don't. And when you ask their reasons for not wanting to give recycled H_2O a go, number one tends to be number twos, and number two is number ones. (Yes, I am often accused of resorting to toilet humour for cheap laughs, but for once it is actually appropriate.)

The idea of drinking water that has already been through someone else leaves a bad taste in most people's mouths. And I understand that. Imagine saying at a bar, 'Wow, this Guinness is delicious' only to be told, 'Ah, sir, that's actually the complimentary tap water!' (On the upside, when you get someone a glass of water at home you'll be able to proudly say, 'I made this.')

But seriously folks, people are getting really hysterical. It's not as if the bidet is suddenly going to start doubling as a bubbler. Personally, I don't get what all the fuss is about. People are willing to put disgusting things in their mouth all the time. How else do you explain the popularity of soy milk? I find it hilarious that people get so upset by the idea of drinking recycled effluent, but will happily eat a Chiko Roll.

I don't want to sound like I'm taking the piss — although that's what all of us will be doing if these laws are passed; in fact, we'll be taking the wee-wee all the way home — but the simple truth is that all the water on the planet is recycled. Is dam water that much cleaner? Fish are having sex in that water. (Although at least they don't have to argue over who gets to sleep on the wet spot.)

Luckily, there's a percentage of the population who don't give a crap, which, if nothing else, will certainly make it a lot easier to clean the water for drinking.

It seems the federal government is going to try and pass a motion through parliament regardless of public opposition — although I'm not sure 'pass a motion' is the best choice of phrasing. As yet there are no firm dates.

Anyhoo, once this is done they'll need to sell the idea to the public. Maybe they need to appeal to our patriotism; perhaps they should change the line in the national anthem to 'Australians all let us rejoice, for we are girt by wee!' Or maybe they just need to think outside the cubicle. Sure, some people are turned off by the idea that their drinking water may have been through someone else's kidney, but what if this was actually the selling point? 'Evian may be French and wet, but this water has gone through Cate Blanchett!'

Another option would be to follow the lead of alcohol companies when they're trying to flog an unpopular brand,

and come up with a range of new designer cocktails, such as the Wee Breeze or Penis Colada. We could even have a Harvey Wallbanger, with real Harvey; or a Margarita where all the ingredients are supplied by Marge and Rita. (And for the kids, why not freeze the water for a delicious poopsicle?)

If all else fails, years of watching TV has taught me one thing, Aussies will swallow any crap if it is delivered in the voice of that bloke from the VB ads. I can see it now: 'You can get it having a laugh, you can get it draining the bath, you can even get it from full-flush or half.' (Calling it Wee-B would probably be a step too far.)

Because something does need to be done about our country's dire water problem. The drought has reached such crisis levels that country pubs are having dry T-shirt contests. Yep, if the rain in Spain falls mainly on the plain, then the rain in Australia is a complete and utter failure.

Sadly, for our long-suffering people on the land, our once sunburnt country is now browner than Jamie Durie after a trip to the solarium. The earth is so parched it resembles a close-up of Paul Hogan's face, and the cracks are so big that when a farmer calls his dog, the echo can last a fortnight.

The drought has become so bad that when rural couples have a 'special cuddle', they don't argue over who has to sleep on the wet spot, they try to plant a crop in it.

You know things are going badly in the country when you squeeze a cow's teat and powdered milk comes out.

Network Ten has even had to stop showing its 9 am talkshow in country areas, because the farmers get teary when they see David Reyne.

We all have to deal with water restrictions, but I don't think most politicians appreciate just how bad things are outside the capital cities. Most of them still seem to think El Niño is the secret identity of Antonio Banderas in *The Mask of Zorro*. You don't believe me? Well, when our former PM was asked about El Niño he said, 'We will decide who comes to this country and the circumstances in which they come.'

I guess they must be listening to those scientists who still don't believe that humans are responsible for global warming – they're usually the ones who got their degrees from the same place as Dr Dre, Dr Feelgood and the Fremantle Doctor. Put it this way, we are mostly talking people whose qualifications wouldn't get them a job at the Ponds Institute.

These 'scientists' tend to counter the claims about climate change with compelling arguments like, 'Nyah, nyah, nyah, I'm not listening', 'I know you are, but what am I?' and 'Well, I've watched the Bundy ads, and that polar bear seems quite happy in the heat. Maybe the rest of them should just chillax a bit and Bundy on!'

Seriously, I'm convinced most of the pollies who listen to these dills reckon that global warming is a good thing because when the polar icecaps melt the ensuing tidal waves will completely solve the drought. (Not to mention suddenly giving Canberra prime beachside property.) These city-slickers seem convinced that thin cows are good because they'll produce milk with less calories. They don't seem to get that in the country, things are so dire that teenage boys are now having dry dreams.

The good news is, we can all make a difference. I try to save water every day. I've been eating my Cup-a-Soup straight from the packet, and if I want tea, I just suck on the bag. I've even started showering with a bucket – although, in retrospect, it might have been a good idea to first take out the KFC. But on the upside, when I poured the soapy water on the garden it cleared up my bougainvillea's dandruff. When I need my car washed I don't take a shower that day. I just put on a pair of Speedos and drive through the local carwash with all my windows down.

Of course, there are some people who don't quite get it. I have a mate who told me he's trying to save water by spending only three minutes in the bath. And look, I admit saving water isn't always easy and you will encounter some resistance. For example, they say you should share a shower with another person. Yet when I broke into Cate Blanchett's bathroom, her husband called the police. I guess he doesn't care about the environment as much as I do. (And I'm pretty sure the restraining order they served me wasn't printed on recycled paper.)

(By the way, even though they say the more plants you grow, the better the environment, the cops will not accept this as an excuse when they find your secret stash in the attic.)

But try as we might, it's becoming increasingly clear that traditional water-saving methods aren't going to be enough. We're all going to have to get a lot more creative. Perhaps farmers should invite the local CWA members to their farm for dinner, make them watch *Beaches* and then get the cows to lick the tears off their faces. Better still, they could invite the participants of a footy end-of-season trip, and after a night of heavy drinking get them to take a leak on the crops. Although, given the high alcohol content in their urine, they might end up with a crop of barley that yells, 'Show us ya tits!'

I read the other day that it is now compulsory for nightclubs to give their patrons free water. Maybe we should take a busload of farmers down to the city and arm them with happy pants, glow sticks, lollipops and buckets.

Or here's an idea: remember being asked to 'bring a plate' to a party? Perhaps we should extend this idea to new migrants, but ask them to bring a jug. Forget the new Aussie Values Test, if you really want entry into the lucky country, you'd better bring a big bottle of Evian. 'Well, Mr Bin Laden, I see you have absolutely no qualifications and a long criminal record, but you've brought a six-pack of Mount Franklin, so you're in!'

We could even change the new tourism slogan from, 'Where the bloody hell are you?' to 'Australia: just add water!'

While we're thinking of ways to attract people to our shores, I wonder if we could get any mileage out of the fact that Australia was recently named the fattest country in the world.

Perhaps something like: 'Come to Australia. By Comparison You'll Feel Instantly Slim!'

Cool. What an honourable award. Did we get a trophy? And more importantly, did it have chocolate inside? And who made the acceptance speech? Did it go something like, 'I would like to thank Krispy Kreme, without whom none of this would be possible. And of course, who could forget our inspirations, Ronnie and the Colonel? A lot of people ask, how did we do this? And I say, while a Mars a day helps you work, rest and play . . . if you don't work or play it just makes you a fat bastard. We're number one, Aussie Aussie Aussie, Oink Oink Oink!'

Yes, ladies and gentlemen, we used to be girt by sea, now we are girth by sea. Maybe the ocean levels aren't rising after all: maybe Australia is sinking because of all the fatty-fatty boombahs.

Australians have apparently become so chubby that the bloodnut who hosts the NRL *Footy Show* has had to change his name to Skinny Vautin.

Now, many in the media got upset about this news, but I think it's a great thing. I mean, when Ian Thorpe wins a gold medal at the Olympics, we're always quick to say things like, 'Go Australia! We're number one. Aren't we good at swimming?'

The truth is, the Thorpedo winning a race doesn't make us good at swimming, it makes *him* good at swimming. However, when we're named the fattest country in the

SURVIVAL OF THE FATTEST

world, each one of us can look down on our beer gut, man boobs and love handles and think: 'I helped!'

Before you complain that you're just 'big-boned', or retaining water due to the drought or hoping to become a contestant on the next series of *The Biggest Loser*, take a look at the facts. Obesity is becoming a bigger problem than drugs in the land with the massive bulge down under. Forget crack addicts, we've got Big Mac addicts. Maybe we need sniffer dogs at the airports – not to check for people bringing in drugs or fruit, but for those who bring back Krispy Kremes.

So why have we gotten so fat? Well, a lot of people eat when they're stressed, so maybe there's just more stress in Australian society. And then people get stressed about being overweight and eat even more.

What's the solution? Maybe the rising price of petrol is a good thing. It might encourage more people to start walking to work. In fact, if we could just get the boffins to come up with a way to power cars on the fat sucked out through liposuction, we could solve two problems at once.

Better yet, how about hooking up the power supply to stationary exercise bikes at gyms: that way we could help the overweight and the environment at the same time.

All jokes aside, with the rising cost of jet fuel there have been calls to disallow overweight people from taking too much luggage on planes. While I understand the logic, this seems a bit cruel to me. I can't imagine getting to the counter and hearing, 'I'm sorry sir, you've already got your excess baggage with you . . . it's called your love handles. And if you could please store your man boobs in the overhead locker, we would really appreciate it.'

Maybe we need to be more creative. Obviously childhood obesity is the major issue we face, so what about getting rid of speed restriction zones around schools? I'll tell you something for free, there won't be too many fat kids if they have to constantly run out of the way of out-of-control 4WDs. Either that, or on school photo day tell them their photographer is Bill Henson.

Here's another idea. We constantly hear that the world is full of starving people (and no, I'm not just talking about contestants on *Australia's Next Top Model*). So why don't we solve two problems at once? Instead of simply sponsoring these malnourished kids, why don't we team them up with a person who needs to lose weight, to act like 'food bodyguards'? That way, every time the fat person attempts to stuff their mouth with something delicious and fattening, the hungry kid simply jumps in front and takes the food. Crisis solved.

Okey-doke, with that whale problem out of the way, let's now turn our attention to those other, far more beautiful, creatures who are being brutally slaughtered by Japanese whalers.

When I heard about this I seriously got so riled up that despite my pathological hatred of bumper stickers, I considered getting one that said, 'Save the Whales'. The thing that really got my goat was the complete manipulation of the truth, with what is clearly commercial whaling disguised as 'scientific research'. I think most people with an IQ slightly higher than that of George W. Bush realised that the only 'scientific research' being conducted on these magnificent mammals was whether they tasted better with wasabi or soy and ginger.

The equivalent would be a bunch of Aussie scientists down at the lab saying, 'Now, forget the groundbreaking cancer research for a minute, I have to do some important scientific research on this Big Mac to see if it really does have two all-beef patties, special sauce, lettuce, cheese ...'

I found the scientific research argument as hard to swallow as a McWhale with extra blubber. I'd seen the horrible footage on the news, and not once did I notice a whaler wearing a lab coat or even holding a Bunsen burner.

Like thousands of Australians, over the years I've really enjoyed Dr Karl's entertaining angle on science and have watched his shows many times; yet I have never seen him slaughter a whale to prove a scientific point. Did the Japanese really think we're gullible enough to believe this? What next? 'Oh no, we're not killing the whales. They're jumping on board voluntarily so they can participate in scientific research.'

As far as I could tell, part of the problem stemmed from the Japanese whalers doing their dirty work in water over which we claimed to have jurisdiction, but which wasn't recognised by the rest of the world. Or, to put it in layman's terms, we called 'dibs' on the ocean and the international courts didn't recognise the time-honoured legal precedent of 'shotgun' or, as it is sometimes known, 'finders keepers, losers weepers'.

However, I did wonder whether declaring this part of the ocean a whale sanctuary was misleading the whales and attracting them to the area. When I hear 'sanctuary' it conjures peaceful images of saunas and yoga. I wouldn't expect to be stabbed with a spear and then spend hours dying painfully. Were we luring whales with the false promise of relaxing massages? (And just a question: when a whale gets a massage, do they listen to human songs?)

At the time, some people argued that the Japanese should be entitled to hunt whales for traditional and food-related reasons, and I could see their point. But what I objected to was the cruel and unusual slaughter. I reckon there should be a rule: if you can hook a whale using nothing but a tinny, a fishing rod and some bait, you can catch as many as you like.

Of course, some Japanese accused us of being hypocrites, because while we were against them catching whales, we're happy to eat cows. Insofar as they are both living creatures, I can accept that argument. But let's be real here. Equating a whale and a cow is so ridiculous that I won't acknowledge it until I see a Japanese person milking a whale.

Although I have to confess, I do sometimes get confused about where we draw the line. For example, tuna manufacturers often advertise 'dolphin-free tuna', but I can't help thinking,

SURVIVAL OF THE FATTEST

that's great, but what about the poor tuna? Surely if the company really cared they would advertise 'tuna-free tuna' – which would, in effect, be an empty can. Or I'm sure the tuna would be happy to settle for 'tuna-free dolphin'.

Then there are the companies that advertise 'dolphin-friendly tuna', apparently promoting the idea that you are eating tuna that were great mates with the dolphins, inviting them around to eat krill and watch old episodes of *Flipper*.

The theory seems to be that it's OK to eat tuna, but it's not OK to eat dolphins, because dolphins are smart. On that logic, if you were a cannibal it would be inappropriate to snack on Stephen Hawking, but you could eat Paris Hilton. (In fact, I think I've seen that video on the internet.)

All jokes aside, I think it's time that, as a civilised society, we stood up and said no to whaling once and for all.

Another thing that's been concerning me is this increasingly bizarre weather we've been having. Yes, we've talked about the drought, but in some parts of the country there are floods. I wouldn't be surprised if next month we had swarms of frogs and locusts.

And let's not forget the wind. Where I live, a few months ago it was windier than sharing a room with Shane Warne when he's on one of his baked-beans-only diets. When we were cleaning up the backyard after the storms we found the *Pasha Bulker* in our swimming pool and a girl stuck in a tree clicking her red shoes together and chanting, 'There's no place like home!'

FRIENDLY FIRE

The weather is undoubtedly getting out of control. A sure sign that we're in trouble is when the wacky weather person on breakfast TV starts filing their reports from the Bureau of Meteorology using graphs and diagrams, rather than from the back of a mechanical bull while a thousand pensioners line-dance around a cake they've baked in the shape of David Koch.

Are we approaching Armageddon? Will it soon be the end of the world as we know it?

If we have only a few years left on this fragile planet, these are the things I'd like to witness before I close my eyes for the last time. A final wish-list, if you like.

I'd like to see Kevin Rudd stop pretending he's in some sort of prime ministerial *Amazing Race* and actually spend time in Australia. There's something wrong when Chris Isaak is in this country more often than the PM.

I want to see Ben Cousins play an entire season, win the Brownlow Medal, and then retire – only for the AFL to drive him around the white line on Grand Final day in a giant nose.

I hope Baz Luhrmann decides to make a sequel to *Australia* called *Australia 2*, about the Aussies taking out the America's Cup, and starring Hugh Jackman as John Bertrand and Bryan Brown as the yacht.

I want to live to see a musical tribute to the first black US president called *Obama-Rama*. And a kids' show starring his daughters called *Obamas in Pyjamas*. It's sad that Obama has to deliver his speeches from inside protective glass walls to prevent assassination, so I hope they decide to have some fun with it and fill the box with money. Whatever he grabs in a minute, he could use to fix the economy.

I want to see the Americans reward George W. Bush for the excellent job he did as their president by sending him on an all-expenses-paid trip to somewhere nice, like Guantánamo Bay.

I'd like to witness Gordon Ramsay's wife finding it in her heart to forgive him for sampling a saucy side dish, but only after he eats humble pie (preferably served by the Coogee Bay Hotel).

I'd like to see the gang from *High School Musical* hit Schoolies' Week and really have some fun.

I also want to see Todd McKenney replace Mark Taylor as the face of air-conditioners, with the slogan: 'Keep your house so cool, you'll never have to take off your pants at a party again.'

And wouldn't it be great if George Michael would just learn to go to the toilet before he leaves the house?

In a bid to make the pre-game show more entertaining in my last years, I want the AFL to combine team banners with the Nine Network's *Hole in the Wall*, so players have to squeeze through various shapes to take to the field.

Before I die, I want the various sporting codes to put Barry Hall, Andrew Symonds, Greg Bird and Wayne Carey in the same room, and whoever makes it out alive is allowed to play again. Or maybe Hall could quit football and become one of

Rudd's advisers, so every time the PM uses the term 'working families', he punches him in the face.

I want former WA Liberal leader Troy Buswell to land a new job as a dog on *Border Security*. If anyone can sniff out plane seats to find out who's smuggling drugs, he can.

I hope I live to see the government admit that the major cause of climate change is publishing 600-page reports about climate change.

And before we all drown in our homes, I'd like to see Australia have another summit, but at this one, all the best and brightest have to gather for a game of cricket while our cricketers come up with ideas for the future (however short a future that is).

I want to see Qantas cash in on its crappy year by advertising a surprise skydiving experience.

I want the government to rethink its decision on internet censorship after realising that under the new guidelines, if someone types 'dick' into Google, the only image they'll find is of a politician.

Before I die, I hope the new Australian Sex Party manages to sustain an election.

Oh, and could someone quickly appoint Larry Emdur as governor of the Reserve Bank? So when they talk about interest rates, he says, 'Lower . . . lower . . . lower.'

Finally, after declaring a war on drugs (didn't work), a war on whalers (didn't work), a war on pokies (didn't work), a war on executive salaries (didn't work), and a war on teen unemployment (didn't work) my last wish is for Rudd to declare a war on hot women giving free stuff to stand-up comedians and magazine columnists.

If you liked *Friendly Fire*, you're going to love Wil's first book, *Survival of the Dumbest*. Read on for a preview.

SURVIVAL OF THE DUMBEST

Sometimes I think we have stopped evolving as a human race. If you need evidence simply read the instructions on the back of almost anything you buy.

I purchased a packet of peanuts the other day, and just reading the labelling made me despair for humanity.

First it was the big bold letters that said: 'Warning, may contain traces of nuts' – well duh – but it was the second line that really pushed me over the edge.

It simply read: 'Instructions, open packet, eat nuts'. Phew, lucky they put that there, I was going to stick them up my butt and then ask someone to pull my finger and do my impression of a poker machine paying out.

But it's not just nuts that have gone nuts. I bought a glass biscuit jar the other day, and it came with instructions. Think about that. Instructions. I'm sorry, but if you need instructions to open a jar, I don't think you should be trusted with glass.

Is there truly anyone who looks at a jar with a lid on it and thinks: 'But how do I get the bikkies in there? It must be some kind of combination, or magic trick. Damn, I wish this thing had instructions.'

Maybe the people who need that kind of help are also those who buy the deodorant I use. The one that has the warning on the back in big letters that says: 'Do not spray in eyes!'

❋ ❋ ❋

Okay, here's my first question . . . who has sweaty eyes? What moron gets up in the morning and thinks: 'Gee my eyes stink . . . ow, ow, ow there should be a warning!'

I don't mean to sound harsh, but if you need that warning, you're too stupid to read it. (Especially if you have previously sprayed deodorant in your eyes.)

You think that warning is stupid? I got some sleeping pills for an overseas flight once, and on the packet it said: 'Warning, may cause drowsiness!'

Really? Well I'd better have a couple of cups of coffee and some Red Bull to take the edge off then.

That's like having a packet of Aspirin that reads: 'Warning, may relieve the symptoms of a headache' or a packet of Viagra that says 'Warning, may cause Grandpa to chase Grandma around the kitchen table.'

There is actually an electric power drill that comes with the warning: 'Not to be used as a dental drill!'

Yes, it's time for *RPA* meets *Better Homes And Gardens*: 'Look, we have used the drill for the pergola, now let's use it for that troublesome molar.' I'm sorry, but if you need that information on your power-tool, then you are a power-tool.

Or the hair-colouring that comes with the instruction: 'Do not use as an ice-cream topping.' Although to be honest, if you are stoned enough to think that is a good idea, you are probably stoned enough to eat it too. Maybe you are happy to eat in a restaurant where there is hair in the food, you just draw the line at it being grey ones.

Of course, if this really happens, then maybe the opposite is true too. That would explain Ray Martin's hair. Maybe it's just Chocolate Ice-Magic.

Then there was the Pepper Spray that apparently comes with the disclaimer: 'Caution, never aim spray at your own eyes.' Now I have to admit, this does sound like sensible advice. Although I also think if you did spray it in your own eyes, it would warn off your attacker, because they would think you were completely nuts. (And if they did still attack you, at least you wouldn't see them coming.)

Hair-dryers now come with the warning: 'Do not use while taking a shower!' Again I feel like this one falls under heading of moron – at the very least because using it while in the shower must limit its effectiveness. 'I have it on high, but for some reason my hair is still wet!'

This is right up there with the toilet brush that comes with the warning sticker: 'Do not use orally!'

Okay, first, unless you have teeth the size of Larry Emdur, who thinks a toilet brush is a good idea for dental hygiene? I don't care if your toothpaste has whitening, tartar control, baking soda, peroxide and bleach in it – that is still not okay. And second, I have heard of teeth smelling like crap, but come on. What's next, using the toilet duck to gargle?

And let's not forget the cigarette lighter that comes with the advice: 'Do not use near open flame.' You see, I would have thought that would be a much better warning to have on Michael Jackson's face.

I don't have an iPod Shuffle, but according to friends who do, they come with the warning that you shouldn't eat them.

Why would anyone eat their iPod? Do you listen to it, and then think, well I know it makes my ears feel good, I wonder how it would make my tongue feel?

Maybe people just see the band names Cake, Ice-Cream Hands, Reel Big Fish and Bread . . . and just can't resist.

One of my favourites was the dishwasher that came with the instruction: 'Don't allow children to play in the dishwasher.' Although, I guess as long as you provided them with some snorkels it would be a pretty quick way to get them clean. But please, whatever you do, don't dry them off in the oven. Use the microwave, it's much quicker.

Speaking of the kiddies, I also hear that Fruit Roll-ups come with the instruction to 'remove plastic before eating'. Although personally I'm not sure I could tell the difference. I don't even buy Roll-ups anymore – I just get a piece of Glad Wrap and colour it in with texta. (Again, if you need this warning you probably also need one on a Kinder Surprise reminding people not to eat the toy.)

And apparently there is a quite popular brand of Baby Oil that has a warning that says: 'Keep away from children.' Yes, you wouldn't want to use the Baby Oil on babies. It's only for fully grown men who dress in nappies and like to coat themselves in the stuff and be spanked.

Maybe they're hiding something more sinister. I mean, they make macadamia oil out of macadamias, and they make hazelnut oil out of hazelnuts ... all I am saying is do the maths. Maybe they just get a bunch of infants down the factory and fire up the blender.

(Or p'raps the problem is that they are worried if George W. finds out the babies have oil, the new Axis of Evil will be Iran, North Korea and Kindergarten.)

But without doubt, my absolute, absolute favourite was the mattress that came with the warning: 'Do not attempt to swallow.'

(There is no truth to the rumour that this is what Matt Shirvington has written on the front of his running shorts.)

Now this warning disturbs and amuses me for a couple of reasons. First, it is so random that you know the only reason it is there is because someone has tried. Secondly, how stoned do you have to be before you try and eat a mattress?

I mean, there are not enough marijuana-filled boogie-board bags in the world to make me try and eat a mattress. How dry would it be? Well, I guess unless you washed it down with a waterbed, and maybe a little hair-dye on top for flavour.

Idiocy is all around us – you just have to open your Lynx-scented eyes. I'll give you another example. I was waiting for a bus the other day, and I noticed on the driver's window there is a little sign that says: 'Do not access bus through window!'

Who is that sign for? Keanu Reeves? People who were born by caesarean and so never go through doors, only through the window? Do they have one on the roof that says: 'Do not access bus by sky-diving'?

Ladies and gentlemen, the simple truth is that there are a lot of simple people in the world.

If you need any further proof, check this out. I read once that in the last ten years, 31 Australians have died from watering the Christmas tree while the lights were still plugged in. What's worse, at least a couple of those were watering plastic trees.

Now I don't want to seem callous, but to me that's not a tragedy – that's natural selection.

You see, from what I can vaguely recall from science at school when we weren't sitting up the back trying to work out how to turn various household items into a bong, there was this bloke called Charles Darwin who came up with the theory of evolution. (And to reward him they named the least evolved city in Australia in his honour.)

In basic terms, it was a matter of Survival of the Fittest. In every generation the strongest and the most intelligent would survive, they would breed together and we would evolve. Well, no more. We have stopped evolving as a human race.

Don't believe me? We live in a time where George W. Bush is the leader of the free world. This is a man Forrest Gump would have hung shit on at school. A man who once said: 'The question is rarely asked, is our children learning?' Most presidents travel on Air Force One, he has to travel on a special bus where they let him lick the windows.

It's no longer Survival of the Fittest, it's Survival of the Dumbest.

And why have we stopped evolving? Well it's simple, all these warnings are keeping the morons alive. And today I have three words for you ladies and gentlemen: Let . . . them . . . go.

I'm serious, if you honestly have a friend who buys a brand new pair of sneakers, gets them home, unpacks them, gets that little package of chemicals out of them and wants to eat them . . . you let them.

It's one less moron to be pissing in the shallow end of our gene pool and we can get back to evolving.

❂ ❂ ❂

Signs and labelling pander to the already dumb, but there are whole industries that depend on drawing out the dumbarse in all of us. Like product development and advertising.

For example, can we just skip to a razor that has a hundred blades and be done with it? I mention this because I noticed the other day one of the major shaving companies is about to launch a new razor with five blades.

That's right, five blades. Apparently the first one picks up the hair, the second cuts it, the third goes out and picks up your dry-cleaning, the fourth goes to market and the fifth goes 'wee wee wee all the way home'.

So the question has to be asked, just how many blades does one man need? If they keep going at this rate, pretty soon I'll have a blade for every single hair on my face.

Put it this way, you know you're in trouble when even Edward Scissorhands thinks you should slow down. I mean, come on, even Wesley Snipes stopped at three Blades.

(Yes, two movie jokes in a row, this column will be killing the all-important video-store clerk demographic.)

But seriously folks, why could we possibly need five different blades on a razor?

Are razors like boy-bands now? You have to have the blade that can sing, the blade that can dance, the ugly blade, the nerdy blade and the gay blade.

I'm all for progress, but it seems to me any more than one blade is a little unnecessary.

I mean unless the other blades are plucking your eyebrows,

trimming your nose and ear hair, and manicuring your bikini line — it seems that one could do the job just fine.

I think it's sad when there are more blades on my razor than in my entire kitchen. These days I'm better off preparing dinner in the bathroom.

It's a vicious cycle. One company adds a blade, so the other adds an extra blade, so then the first company has to add another blade, and that's pretty much how the Cold War started.

What's next, the Gillette Tomahawk, with fifty blades and extra uranium to make sure your hair never grows back?

Maybe Kim Jong Il isn't interested in pursuing a nuclear arms race, maybe he's just interested in keeping his mad dictator's face as smooth as a baby's bottom.

And while I am having my razor rant, who is naming these things? You have The Mach, The Fusion, The Champion, The Turbo, and The Quatro.

It sounds less like the names of razor blades and more like a casting call for a new series of Gladiators.

At the moment I'm using a Mach Turbo, which sounds like something Mark Webber should be driving in the Formula One Grand Prix.

And now I see you can get razors with batteries, that vibrate, and even have something called a 'lubra-strip'.

Let's face it, if they can come up with a razor that gives a good foot massage and plays James Blunt, pretty soon women won't need men at all.

And have you ever read the packaging on these things? My current razor is a Gillette which, according to the blurb, is 'the best a man can get'.

Really? Personally I would have thought any sentence that talked about the 'best a man can get' would have also included the words 'Scarlett Johansson' and 'lap-dance'.

Who wrote that slogan, Dr Seuss? 'Gillette, it's the best a man can get, and if you use it on your pet, you should take them to the vet.'

But I digress. The one thing that shocked me most of all when I read the back of my razor packet is that my razor has its own website. Yes, that's right, I'll repeat that again, my razor has its own website.

I guess that's not the site most people are expecting when they type 'hot' and 'shaved' into Google.

(They will be even more shocked when they type in 'big jugs' and end up at www.tupperware.com.)

But think about this for a moment. With all the infinite possibilities offered by the internet, how bored would you have to be to look up the website for a razor blade?

So anyway, I looked it up.

And check this out, not only does my razor have a website, but it also has its own fan-club. I am not making this up.

Now, I'm sorry, but if you are the sort of person who joins a fan-club for a razor blade then you have a lot more serious problems than a little bum-fluff.

In fact if you are the sort of person who would join a fansite for a razor, I'm not sure I want you handling a blade.

I'm not sure you should be trusted with anything that close to your face that isn't made of ice-cream.

I don't know about you, but sometimes it really scares me that we live in a world where nobody could name the most recent winner of the Nobel Prize for Physics, but a razor blade has its own fan-club.

I think I'm just going to give up and grow a beard.